REORGAN

REORGANISE

15 STORIES OF WORKERS
FIGHTING BACK
IN THE DIGITAL AGE

Lucy Harley-McKeown

Copyright © 2022 by Lucy Harley-McKeown

Cover design by Sam Ballard
Cover copyright © 2022 by Sam Ballard

The scanning, uploading and distribution of this book without the author's permission is a theft of their intellectual property. If you would like permission to use any material in the book (other than for review purposes) please contact lucy.hm.work@gmail.com. Thank you for supporting the author's rights.

Printed in the UK.

Published by The London College of Political Technology at Newspeak House, an independent residential college founded in 2015 to study, nurture and inspire emerging communities of practice across UK public sector and civil society.

ABOUT THE AUTHORS

Lucy Harley-McKeown is a journalist who covers business, economics and the world of work. In 2021, she was shortlisted for new freelance writer of the year at the UK Freelance Writing Awards. She is now an editor at The Block.

Edward Saperia is dean of the London College of Political Technology at Newspeak House, an independent residential college founded in 2015 to study, nurture and inspire emerging communities of practice across UK public sector and civil society.

Hannah O'Rourke is Director of the political network Labour Together, a network for people from all traditions of the Labour movement explore new ideas and thinking on the future of the left.

The work was copy edited by Kirsty Styles, a journalist, campaigner, researcher and performer, advocating for good information, ethical technology and diverse leadership.

To my parents

CONTENTS

Foreword by Jon Cruddas MP — IX
Preface — XV
Introduction — XXI

1. The Turkopticon: *organising the invisible internet workforce you've never heard of* — 31
2. Lads and Gangs: *how construction workers use a Facebook Group to set their own terms* — 42
3. Glassdoor: *how a million-dollar corporation went to court to protect anonymous worker whistleblowers* — 50
4. Crowdjustice and #DoNotPay: *how new platforms are giving workers access to justice* — 58
5. Worker Info Exchange: *how to fight back when your boss is an algorithm* — 65
6. #PublishingPaidMe: *how hashtag activism changed the tide on industry discrimination* — 71
7. SpoonStrike: *how a group chat took on a pub giant* — 79

8.	Fuck you, Pay Me: *how Instagram influencers are standing up for creators*	84
9.	Organise: *a new platform for workers to take action together*	91
10.	WeClock: *how new technology is tackling the multi-ion dollar 'wage theft' problem*	98
11.	The Grapevine: *how TV and film workers bootstrapped a union*	107
12.	United Tech and Allied Workers: *how tech workers are building tools to rebel against surveillance*	113
13.	The FUNemployed: *how a minimum wage was set by a Facebook group*	120
14.	EveryDoctor: *how young medics built a new institution after the junior doctors' strike*	127
15.	#FreelancerPayGap and Journo Resources: *Epilogue: How writers are building power by pooling data*	134

Acknowledgements	143
Glossary	147
Notes	149

FOREWORD

Over recent decades work has been de-coupled from politics. Much literature on work side-steps political questions regarding the deployment of labour. The type of the work we do and why we do it has come to be understood as a personal choice, a trade-off between work and leisure, rather than a political one.

This was not always the case. Historically, the forms by which labour was understood as an economic and political category, together with how it was deployed, regulated and represented underpinned alternative approaches to how society should itself be organised - competing theories of justice - and dominated politics.

Yet, recently, the politics of work appears to be changing.

On the right, Boris Johnson has begun to argue that

Britain needs a new economic model. In his 2021 Conference speech, he announced it was time to tackle the "long-term structural weaknesses" of the UK economy, and, after 11 years in government, plans for a policy overhaul to a "high-wage, high-skill, high-productivity economy". This reorientation was best represented on 2 February 2022 when the government published its long-awaited 'Levelling Up' White Paper.

Yet, in reality, the Conservatives have shown a marked reluctance to implement the kind of employment and labour market reforms signalled in the ultimately inadequate Taylor Review of Modern Working Practices[1] – a report published in July 2017. There is little beyond political rhetoric.

On the left Labour in general continues to inhabit a post-Brexit stasis, seemingly trapped by the political binaries of age, education, geography, and the effects of the 2016 referendum. Yet over recent months it, too, has begun to show renewed interest in how labour is deployed and regulated.

In the summer of 2021 Labour launched a 'new deal for working people' campaign which pledged to "fundamentally change our economy" and "make Britain the best place to work". Starmer reinforced the message in a speech to the 2021 TUC Congress where he declared a future Labour government would deliver a new deal for workers – in particular his party would enforce full rights and protections for all workers from their first day in a job.

Such political reorientations can be interpreted as responses to populist threats that threaten liberal democracy alongside the effects of the pandemic. Politicians are tacitly recognising that the indignities central to modern work pose a threat to capitalism itself; its failure to deliver rewarding, satisfying labour.

Moreover within a few months of the onset of the pandemic, human labour was politicised in ways thought unimaginable throughout the preceding decades. The market for labour stopped. The role of the state vis-à-vis labour was redefined. A Tory government had to step in and regulate who works, where and under what conditions. The TUC re-emerged at the centre of economic life for the first time in over 40 years and helped to forge the most significant labour market intervention of living memory: a state furlough programme covering some 11 million workers.

So this refocus on the politics of work is welcome. But something big is missing – the voice of the people themselves; the political agency of those at the sharp end.

If work is being transformed and remains important beyond providing us with material subsistence – central to our overall human wellbeing – then what do the workers themselves think and how can they organise? If modern work patterns are being upended and people's identities based on their labour are being transformed in an age that is characterised for many by precariousness, declining material reward and flat-lining social mobility, with intensifying digitalisation, job rotation and meaningless labour, then what do those workers themselves understand and feel about these changes and how can they influence them?

This book begins to fill a huge gap in our understanding. It provides much needed original research into the modern world of work. It is a deeply democratic intervention – giving voice to the political voiceless. It is highly political – identifying and nurturing new forms of political organisation and agency. It is de-stabilising for much of the traditional left forged on post war patterns of work organisation and representation. It is an insurgent work – challenging and at times uncomfortable for those brought up within the traditional political discourses of the left. Above all it is fascinating in terms of the way it builds a portal into our modern world – a world way beyond Westminster and the orthodox terms of political debate.

The practical application of this work cannot be understated – especially the way tech savvy activists are challenging the architecture and power of algorithms, creating powerful networks and communities from below to take back power and control, how radical appropriation of technologies can liberate and humanise modern work and contest and push back against the invasive powers of these technologies. It challenges both deterministic views of technology and their perceived neutrality – it re-establishes the inherently contested terrain of technology and work. And it retains a rich, funny counterculture strain; a hallmark of the radical left often drowned out by the dominant utilitarian Labour cultures.

This book – with its stories of influencers, road workers and strikers; the unemployed, health workers, journalists, writers and freelancers, is a wonderfully humane, original contribution that will incubate new forms of political discussion and mobilisation.

The best political interventions are often iconoclastic; demanding. As a Labour MP of a certain age - the product of union and political cultures a world away from these – this collection is a destabilising, unnerving read.

I hope it helps upend politics and shape a different future.

In the past the study of labour was fundamental to both political philosophy and the day to day practice of politics. Yet in recent decades politics has withdrawn from these political traditions. It is a withdrawal that has come at great cost, for it has truncated our moral critique of capitalism and limited our capacity to organise and resist. So whilst Reorganise is a deeply modern book it can be situated in the best radical traditions of the left concerned with power, democracy and human liberation. It is a great humanist contribution.

Jon Cruddas MP
20 May 2022

PREFACE

> *Thousands of road workers assembling in a Facebook group, a subreddit of the invisible clickworkers that hold the internet together, a network of Uber drivers reverse-engineering the algorithm that controls them.*

> *Workers are reorganising.*

The cut and thrust of the political news cycle can make it easy to miss more complex changes happening in the lives of workers. While many are aware that the dramatic changes to the economy have brought with them stories of exploitation, workplace strikes, oppressive workplaces and falling wages, much less attention has been paid to the new ways that workers are fighting back. Under the radar, away from the mainstream, something new is emerging.

For the last decade, we have been researching how technology affects civic and political movements. In our exploration, we have discovered a growing number of examples of workers organising in unusual ways, both within existing trade unions and beyond them. In this book we present some of these stories to make visible these important but little-investigated sites of struggle, which we hope will inform essential conversations about today's, and tomorrow's, labour movement.

Workers' movements are often dismissed as being suspicious of technology. Yet the stories in this book show in practice they are using technology to create new ways for people to work together to make change. What can be tools of oppression may be turned into tools of resistance. Technology can dehumanise and automate, but it can also be used to empower, connect, reconstruct and reclaim.

There is a lot of variety and experimentation. Some groups repurpose popular tools like WhatsApp or Google Docs in unusual ways. Others build custom software from scratch, sometimes in collaboration with academics. Some worker movements are even funded by venture capital as startup enterprises. Nascent worker institutions, which may not even have names, can find themselves in conflict with established trade unions. There is still no clear settlement between traditional, tried-and-tested approaches to workplace organising, and these newer tools and processes, which might be a thousand-fold faster and more accessible, but also bring new kinds of problems.

This is also not just about efficiency. The changes created by the technological revolution are cultural as well as instrumental, and in fact, the two are tightly interwoven. While there are powerful new tools for collective action, they exist within a prevailing ideology of individual enterprise and atomisation.

For some of us, to complain about work is to jeopardise our livelihood in a competitive world. For many, a lack of financial security is characterised as a personal failing, our anger directed inwards, rather than at an exploitative system. For those working in entirely new roles and industries, such as influencers, they may not yet have the language to articulate the nature of the unfairness they are experiencing. In this context, many workers have struggled to name their concerns and take action, and may not recognise what they are doing as organising.

In many instances, this collective action is not framed as collective at all. Glassdoor, for example, is a platform that collects testimonies about company culture and promises to help workers find good jobs. The site is hugely popular as a place to complain about poor treatment at work. A convenient byproduct is that many bad reviews from individual employees can drive away potential job applicants, and so put pressure on businesses to improve. Individual actions become more than the sum of their parts, as the gathering of many personal data points builds collective power.

As workplace surveillance and automated management become more prevalent, access to the underlying data becomes a significant site of struggle. At its extreme, your working day and rate of pay may be determined by the analysis of vast quantities of data, while the method for doing so is completely opaque. Under such faceless systems of management by algorithm, it may only be through pooling knowledge that workers can begin to understand the rules they are working to in the hope of changing them. This is far from an alternative culture of solidarity – in some cases this type of data-cooperative activism may be entirely anonymous, and a worker may never communicate directly with another colleague.

Where a culture of solidarity does grow, it is likely to be informal, and may begin only as grim in-jokes shared anonymously on an online forum. Here, technology is being used in very human ways to create spaces for sharing collective experiences – it is through this sharing that common understanding is found and ideas for action may stir. The FUNemployed Facebook group provides such a place, where tens of thousands of casual workers share their work experiences, mainly through jokes and rants about bad jobs. Forums like this are as much about building a sense of community as they are about sharing information – helping people feel less alone – in what is often a lonely working world, especially for those without a physical workplace.

But it goes further. The FUNemployed Facebook Group has actually instigated its own minimum wage. When you bring together workers you can also create economic power. The group members own and control the space and how their labour is accessed. They set the terms on which employers can share opportunities, and thus can insist on a minimum wage. Here, fair pay hasn't been achieved by a lengthy union negotiation, or government regulation, but through an informal collective assembling in an online space, facilitated by technology.

As these forums mature, they may spawn powerful new forms of organised worker institutions. These may look very different to what has come before, they may operate in different ways and they may evolve differently. We may not at first recognise them as worker organising. Yet, as capitalism has created, and re-created itself for, the digital age, so too must the workers whose labour underpins it. We hope this book will help to record the early stages of this struggle.

The first industrial revolution resulted in a class consciousness that gave rise to a powerful trade-union movement that still protects millions of workers today. For today's technological revolution, each story here represents a new, collective hope, in action, in times that can feel individually hopeless.

Finally: we know these stories are not exhaustive. There are many interesting experiments in organising going on internationally across the world, which in this book we have not been able to include. Similarly, we know many workers are building power through new cooperative models of ownership which again we have not been able to cover in depth here. Ultimately our stories are examples of a much bigger ecology of workers organising to change the world today, for tomorrow. They may also have evolved or vanished by the time this book is in your hands. We are always looking for more, so if you have examples that you feel should be in our collection, please drop us a line at morestories@reorganise.work

Edward Saperia
Hannah O'Rourke

INTRODUCTION

BUSINESS IS BOOMING, BUT NOT FOR EVERYONE

Some have done really rather well in recent years. In 2020, the first year of the pandemic, 25 of the world's largest publicly traded companies collectively increased their total market value by $5.8 trillion (£4.4 trillion). That's $231 ion (£176 ion) each on average, according to a report[2] by consultancy McKinsey & Company, reflecting shareholder confidence in the future of their work.

In particular, McKinsey points out, the 'Mega 25', full of digital-economy brands we all recognise, were in a category of their own. These valuations put them among the richest countries in the world.

Given such staggering wealth creation, why then, is Oxfam warning[3] that a quarter of a ion more people around the world could be pushed extreme poverty in 2022? And why is the New Economics Foundation suggesting[4] that one in three people in the UK will no longer be able to afford the 'cost of living' this year?

This growth in inequality is linked to the fact that the nature of employment has radically changed in recent years here too. For many, work and life in the UK are less stable than at any time in living memory. So-called 'gig economy' jobs now capture three in every 20 working adults, coming hand-in-hand with a broad erosion of workers' rights.

On top of decades of deregulation and globalisation, the COVID-19 pandemic has prompted a further shove towards a cashless, insecure online economy in the UK. At its peak in February 2021, 36.8% of retail sales were being done online, during some of the most stringent lockdown restrictions in the UK, according to the Office for National Statistics (ONS).[5] The knock-on effect of this has been the need for a lot more capacity, and human labour, in warehouses and supply chains. Amazon's total market value is now well on its way to $2 trillion (£1.6 trillion), while its workers are, in some cases, worse off than ever.

INTRODUCTION

PEOPLE ARE PRECARIOUSLY FREELANCE INSTEAD OF UNEMPLOYED

Recent data from gig-economy recruiter AppJobs shows that freelance labour in the UK is on course to almost quadruple in the next three years[6], continuing on from an initial sharp increase in 2019. This growth in solo self-employment is not confined to low-paid jobs, such as delivery couriers or warehouse workers on zero-hours contracts. Freelance labour also increased among high-paid occupations, such as managers and IT professionals, as well as among hairdressers, cleaners and drivers. The share of workers who are solo self-employed has increased relatively evenly across the wage distribution, according to the Institute for Fiscal Studies (IFS)[7].

The IFS says that this is, in part, a symptom of a lack of opportunity in the traditional employee–employer labour market. These new working arrangements also seem to suppress wages. When looking across countries, and across regions of the UK, areas that see increases in solo self-employment also tend experience slower growth in employee wages. This suggests that the solo self-employed may play a similar role to that of unemployed, providing a 'reserve army' of potential employees, which reduces the bargaining power of existing employees, and hence restrains wage growth.

This environment is also muddied by national employment law – the UK is the only country in Europe to have an intermediate 'worker' category between employee and self-employed – where people are entitled to the minimum wage and holiday pay, but not protected against dismissal or redundancy. There is no tax withholding obligation for this category, meaning they must also look after their own tax affairs.

Even those working full-time, permanent jobs have also been subject to increasingly poor working conditions. Despite many large companies now putting outsized emphasis on employee wellness, research by NordVPN Teams suggests those who work from home were spending longer at their desks and are dealing with a bigger workload than before the pandemic.[8]
Why, then – with a deteriorating working environment – have trade unions, to some extent, fallen by the wayside?

IF IT'S SO BAD TO BE A WORKER, WHY AREN'T UNIONS BOOMING?

Why, then – with a deteriorating working environment – have trade unions, to some extent, fallen by the wayside?

When workers worked in the same place, and banded together, there was record trade-union membership –

in 1979, unions represented 13.2 million UK employees, 53% of all workers.[9] But over the past five years, as more workers have left 'the physical workplace', this has bumped along at historically low levels – at 23.3% of employees in 2017, rising slightly to 23.7% in 2020, or 6.56 million people, according to the latest UK government data.[10] It's unsurprising that disparities in union membership broadly tend towards older rather than younger workers, concentrated in the public rather than the private sector, representing those in longer-term full time jobs rather than short-term part-time staff. People who are in trade unions today are ultimately more likely to be working in sectors that have a strong history of trade unions or where there is already a strong union presence.

Despite these problems, there has been some better news more recently, as the recognition of GMB as an official union for Uber and Deliveroo drivers signals some attempts of traditional unions to represent newer workplaces. A new union, the IWGB was also founded by Latin American cleaners in 2012 to organise precarious workers who are often low paid migrant workers. It operates mainly in sectors such as cleaning, facilities delivery and security services where traditional unions have often found it harder to organise. Similarly, total trade-union membership among employees has risen for four consecutive years following a low of 6.23 million members in 2016. The latest year-on year increase in these figures was driven by growing public-sector membership – coinciding with people organising for better conditions during COVID-19 – but that again reinforces those wider membership trends. To some extent, the state of unions holds up a mirror to the state of work.

As our work has changed, so has our own relationship to work. US economist and labour-market expert David Weil argues that, because big business has largely rejected direct employment, instead emphasising customer satisfaction while outsourcing much of the work, there is no longer a clear-cut, employer-employee relationship.[11] The "responsibility for conditions has become blurred," he says.

This problem is also partially due to the fact that our current understanding of workplace organising is dependent on the current political paradigm.

"We live in a capitalist system which has trained us to see through the eyes of the market, interrogating the value in everything we pay for and viewing those purchases solely as one-way services in the pursuit of acquisition," Eve Livingston writes in her 2021 book *Make Bosses Pay: Why We Need Unions*.[12] Indeed, the price of a company's stock often rises when cost cutting and job losses are announced.

Livingston argues that the way we understand union membership should not be through the lens of just subscription, but through participation – as a gateway for people who want to build and empower. Without a change in mindset, unions will continue to be disempowered, she says.

NEW KINDS OF WORK NEED NEW KINDS OF ORGANISING

> **SAM JEFFERS**
> *"It has to be easy to join a union on the bus on the way home after an argument with your boss."*

As academics and activists have grappled with what to do, new initiatives have sprung up to make membership more attractive. Take the Young Workers' Lab at the UNI Global Union, a global coalition of unions, which says its mission is to explore how digital technologies, data and power can be shared, in order to democratise access to the collective value of the digital age. It's specifically geared towards engaging younger workers, who are underrepresented in traditional union membership.

Other efforts have tried to fix fundamental problems with processes, such as simplifying the membership journey and making it easier to join unions. Campaigner and head of consultancy at The Shop, Sam Jeffers, describes this as bridging a "frictionless digital gap". "It has to be easy to join a union on the bus on the way home after an argument with your boss," he says.

While these initiatives try to encourage membership of traditional unions, other new projects are aiming to return power to workers, in the face of the failings of traditional structures. New ways to organise have broken through, and, in some cases, forced material change – from crowdsourced wage data, to apps tracking burnout and organising via WhatsApp, as well as entirely new platforms and unions created to hold employers to account. These projects represent a decoupling from our traditional understanding of what a union does – they can, at once, harness the power of the collective on specific issues and champion a decentralisation of services in an increasingly fragmented world.

This book is not critical of unions, but seeks to show how some are changing, and may provide a valuable challenge for others. Some of these stories are about how traditional unions are adapting, some are about how new unions are working with older ones and many are about what is emerging pre-figuratively before formal unions. We hope people working in unions will read this book and think about how the traditional institutions of the labour movement can engage with what is emerging – how might they help it grow and formalise, and how might it influence their own practices. We also hope that for anyone hoping to start organising themselves in their own workplaces, this will be a useful collection of stories recording how others have begun to do this.

There's limited understanding of such worker organising, and indeed workplaces, today.

So, that's why we've spent the last year speaking to the people, groups and organisations behind these innovations. What follows is a series of stories that highlight how this existential moment, for work, workers and workers' rights, has kicked people into action. It spans different geographies, and both old and new industries. The following chapters try to tease out what's at the heart of these struggles for change, including where existing organisations and structures have tried, or failed.

There is life in the fight to make work better. This is how workers have re-organised in the 21st century.

THE TURKOPTICON

ORGANISING THE INVISIBLE INTERNET WORKFORCE YOU'VE NEVER HEARD OF

> ANONYMOUS TURKER
>
> *"I am a human being, not an algorithm, and yet employers seem to think I am there just to serve their bidding"*

Ever wondered who makes sure all the links on your bank's website are working? Or checks the product descriptions fit the on shopping websites? Artificial intelligence (AI) might not be as clever as you think – it's people power behind much of what actually makes the internet make sense. Workers who check and update these details are spread out across the world, in different time zones and geographies.

Mechanical Turk is at the heart of this system. It's a marketplace created by Amazon that facilitates 'Human Intelligence Tasks' or HITS. These are small repetitive actions, such as testing websites for bugs, writing descriptions of images, or answering simple questions. Businesses routinely outsource these kinds of jobs to anonymous workers across the globe, who are paid pennies for each task. They are usually checking work that a machine has already done – essentially making the 'intelligence' in AI look like it's performing perfectly. These people call themselves 'Turkers'.

Turking is a type of 'piece work', a practice which took on increased importance during the industrial revolution, from the mid-1700s. At this time, imported American machine-making methods were replacing the older English system of artisans handcrafting items such as clothes. With this shift, the process of producing goods was broken down into the assembly of different "pieces". Workers, rather than being paid a proportion of the overall price for the finished product, instead were paid according to the number of "pieces" they produced within this system.

Today, under UK employment law, piece workers must be paid either at least the minimum wage for every hour worked, or on the basis of a 'fair rate' for each piece of work they do. Yet Turkers working on an international platform as independent contractors are not currently covered by this legislation.

As an employment practice, mechanical turking has been widely criticised. Technology theorist Jaron Lanier noted how the design of Mechanical Turk "allows you to think of the people as software components" and that it conjures "a sense of magic, as if you can just pluck results out of the cloud at an incredibly low cost". By its nature, it sets out a worker-employer relationship where individuals have no ability to negotiate their pay

1 - THE TURKOPTICON

or conditions. Existing unions have struggled to represent these workers, partly due to this lack of visibility, along fact that the workforce is so disparate. That was, until Turkopticon showed up.

Developed by a computer-science academic and a software engineer, this volunteer-maintained platform, dubbed Turkopticon, allows users to give feedback on organisations that request work. This means others can avoid potentially bad jobs and get recommendations for better employers. Turkopticon says it "helps the people in the 'crowd' of crowdsourcing watch out for each other—because nobody else seems to be".

This is done through a piece of code that adds functionality to the Mechanical Turk platform, placing a button next to each requester and highlighting those with reviews from other workers. Bad reviews let those doing the work avoid shady employers and good reviews help them find fair ones, the website says.

> "[Turkers] can view reports made against requesters with a quick click."

This has a real impact for many workers, as demonstrated by this post on the Reddit forum for Turkers[13]

r/mturk
u/floydasaurus · 3y

I love you guys and TurkOpticon so much

Without TO I would have wasted so much damn time on bullshit hits that either take way longer than advertised, pay far too little, have jerkface requesters, or constant rejections for no reason.

Thank you.

Saw the Scalable Play Immediately hit, accepted it.

Read all the TO reviews and Noped right the F out.

acasualfitz · 3y

That's the only way we can teach requesters to be reasonable and pay a fair wage.

Screenshot, accessed 29/07/2022, Reddit

1 - THE TURKOPTICON

A DECADE IN THE MAKING

Turkopticon was originally conceived of by two academics, Lilly C. Irani and M. Six Silberman, in the US. The idea first came to life in 2009, and was built and maintained by them alongside a group of Turkers. An initial survey sent out by the researchers identified eight problems: uncertainty about payment; unaccountable and seemingly arbitrary rejections (i.e., non-payment); fraudulent tasks; prohibitive time limits; pay delays; uncommunicative requesters and administrators; costs of employer errors borne by workers; and low pay.

After defining these problems, the platform was built to help workers fight these conditions. The ultimate plan was always that it would be worker-led and run – a transition that happened a decade later, in 2019 – through phased training. A watershed moment came when the organisation's central servers were shifted away from the university where it was being hosted. This was seen as a huge milestone in its journey towards worker ownership and autonomy.

As part of the tool's development, the group wrote a of Rights, prompted by Irani and Silberman's research. This demanded protection from employers who take the work without paying. The document asks workers to imagine what "better" crowdwork might mean to them.

The solution is intrinsically linked to how Amazon has built humans in as a critical cog of the platform, without getting accountability from employers in return. The pair wrote in a paper in 2013:[14]

> "The very stories about labour that attracted us to design were the same stories that devalued Turkers' work."

> "Stories about "innovation" and "design" conditioned Turkopticon's meaning and its impact on workers. We could only discern this in the long term. It takes time to let meanings develop and stabilize."

> "It takes time to build sufficiently thick relationships with project participants to let critiques of project conveners emerge."

> "It takes time periment with ensembles of responses, including finding different storytelling strategies, rearranging terms of inclusion, and following up with projects that address previous shortcomings."

> "This work and reflection expands the frame of action over half a decade of making, watching, waiting, being surprised, and trying again. We find where the action is stretched out over time, strung together in supply chains in contested systems of value and meaning."

1 - THE TURKOPTICON

Turkopticon is now run by a core team and numerous other volunteers around the world. The distributed nature of this means it can be tricky to run, said a Turkopticon member, who asked not to be named due to the sensitivity of their work. Different time zones, cultures and languages have to be taken into account. It is a job of logistics.

When a new Turker contacts them or asks to work with them, organisers will set up one-to-one meetings to understand their specific issues. This guides future action. They also organise using open community forums and group discussions. A lot of what Turkopticon now does, and the way it is maintained, relies on word of mouth. These workers have organised through subreddits – threads of messages on community content aggregator Reddit – in the past, too. It's in these forums that workers can share their achievements and their frustrations with their work, finding others who understand.

One post on the subreddit r/mturk highlights the difficult nature of some of the requests workers receive, and the lack of fair compensation for this kind of work.
[15]

As well as maintaining and updating the tool, the organisation goes to great lengths to foster a community. The core group manages a newsletter with several thousand subscribers. Again, the content has to be

It's insulting as fuck when requesters want you to take a survey about traumatic events/subjects for extremely low pay.

Of course, all low-paying HITs are annoying, but something seems especially mean and perverse about making people think about their trauma or illness for five cents. Yes, they have IRB forms so you are a knowing participant, but the emotional/psychological risk should be compensated more fairly. For example, when you ask someone 30 questions about their sexual assault or how they feel about their recent cancer diagnosis, the chance of bringing up very dark and potentially damaging thoughts increases. Therefore, the compensation should, too. The research is obviously important, but the emotional wellbeing of people who survived/are currently battling these issues matters, too. If our trauma is going to get you in a top journal or secure your tenure, we should be compensated like it matters to you.

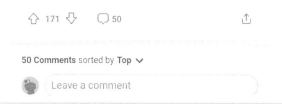

Screenshot, accessed 29/07/2022, Reddit

carefully chosen, due to the global demographic of the people working on the project. The group also has an active social media presence, which they hope to ramp up during 2022.

The future of the group depends on fundraising, so they have to spend time finding grants they can apply for and thinking about new sources of income to fund the maintenance of the platform. They also routinely attend academic conferences to try to facilitate properly representative research into such crowdsourced work.

A MOVEMENT AGAINST AMAZON

Turkopticon sits among a wider movement against Amazon with a number of innovations that seek to hold the company to account on behalf of workers. Another service, called Dynamo, allows Amazon workers to collect information anonymously and organise campaigns to improve their working environment. It works through a plug-in – a software component that adds a specific feature to an existing computer programme.

Amazon has since made it more difficult for workers to use Dynamo. It stopped workers from being able to use the plug-in and installed updates intended to prevent future plug-ins from working. Among other forms of action, these projects have helped spur the production of Guidelines for Academic Requesters in 2014,[16] which provides principles for people allocating HITS work to do so fairly, including rates of pay. These guidelines, however, quickly became outdated, as the work changed and labour laws evolved.

This movement also spawned the 'Dear Jeff Bezos' campaign, where Mechanical Turk workers wrote to Amazon's CEO in protest against their working conditions. "I am a human being, not an algorithm, and yet [employers] seem to think I am there just to serve their bidding," one of the letters stated.[17] The campaign aimed to flood Bezos' email inbox – from which he is known for responding to employees – with their demands. These ranged from asking for a more modern website to find work through, to getting recognition that they are skilled and educated people, not just parts of a machine.

The combination of giving such campaigns a human face, and using data and code strategically, has slowly moved the goalposts for these workers, who are now known as a formidable force by Amazon leadership.

WHAT DOES THIS TELL US?

Turkopticon, and other campaigns that have organised against Amazon, show how even companies that are 'too big to fail' can be held to account by workers through online organising. A critical mass of people asking for better conditions, as well as smart use of data collection tools, can make a meaningful difference. They also show how important it is to provide space, even if it is virtual, for workers to organise and connect with each other.

The fact that this was an academic concept first, but one that quickly brought workers in, demonstrates how important it is to include those affected when putting theory into practice. Turkopticon is still working on improving conditions for employees to this day. "We see the need for this service far into the future, because we do more than just host this website," said an anonymous member of the group.

Turkopticon continues to operate and engage with its growing community of workers. Its current priorities include increasing the visibility of this largely invisible form of work and launching an ongoing fundraising campaign to ensure the future of the project.

Link: *turkopticon.net*

LADS AND GANGS

HOW CONSTRUCTION WORKERS USE A FACEBOOK GROUP TO SET THEIR OWN TERMS

> KEVIN WALSHE, ROAD WORKER AND FACEBOOK GROUP MODERATOR
>
> *"If you try to underpay you just get annihilated in the comments. You have to delete the post."*

Despite its many sins, Facebook has been instrumental in providing a new way for workers in old industries to come together to improve their life at work. Full-time machine operator Kevin Walshe's group, Lads and Gangs, is one such example.

The group – which is used primarily as a tool to help link employers and employees in the construction sector – has in effect, set its own minimum wage, while manufacturing a way to hold employers accountable. It has amassed tens of thousands of members, as well as inspiring multiple sister groups for different parts of the industry.

It is not only a forum for sourcing and distributing work, but also acts as a place where people can share tips and advice related to the industry, building solidarity and joining the dots between workers, who might not otherwise know each other.

One particular challenge in this industry is that often construction companies liquidate without protecting the workers. Sometimes they don't get paid for work they have done, leaving them out of pocket. Some companies have become known for doing this, while others have been able to fly under the radar. "The working man at the bottom often doesn't get paid – but suppliers do," says Walshe. "It's almost like some companies do it on purpose."

Walshe says these groups are important for workers because they operate differently from recruitment websites, such as Indeed or CV-Library – they allow workers to identify and call out bad employers. By sharing information, people are able to issue a warning to others or join forces with those who have not been paid.

A PLACE TO GET HELP AND TO BE REMEMBERED

Started in 2014, the original group was created for UK-based Construction Plant Competence Scheme (CPCS) operators, a subset of construction workers. As news spread about this new way to acquire and advertise work, membership gathered pace.

Screenshot, accessed 29/07/2022, Facebook

2 - LADS AND GANGS

The types of work being advertised expanded, opening up to people that maintain gas, water and electric systems, as well as those working in demolition and more besides. Then came sector focused spin offs, as well as another internationally focused construction group with more than a million members.

A lot of the jobs advertised through Lads and Gangs listings are short term – they could be a few months down to just a couple of weeks. These arrangements suit a lot of people in the group, many of whom are self-employed and may need extra work for a short period of time, says Walshe. The construction industry in the UK could not run without these kinds of contractors.

The group is open to any person in the industry, with posts seen by thousands of people and many getting instant responses. "People who chip in often say, 'that's a bad person to work for because they've done this, that and the other'. If someone is common at late-paying people, then people jump on the posts," says Walshe.

Usually, Walshe and other moderators don't allow posts that quote below a certain fee for a particular job. If something below the average wage does get approved, people will criticise the person posting it in the comments as a matter of course, says Walshe. "If you try to underpay you just get annihilated in the comments. You have to delete the post," says Walshe.

Many construction workers are not in official unions, and as long as this remains the case, Facebook will be an important space to understand going rates and potentially dodgy employers, as well as helping to benchmark workers' rights. This comes with some risks. The platform has tried to shut the group down due to occasional posts that break its rules. Walshe says 99% of the time moderators keep this under control, but a group with more than 100,000 members can be unruly.

Other kinds of posts help people build solidarity and share information about improving their working conditions. Some recommend equipment, such as ear protectors for drilling or advice about the best boots to buy. Others outline the correct ways to signpost things, such as roadworks. It's a handy resource as well as a thriving recruitment tool.

There are even posts commemorating members of the forum who have passed away, including one worker who "helped design and build from scratch, some of the first ever epoxy resin lining rigs" and went on to train many others in the industry. Another eulogises a worker who was a "legend from the cable world".

2 - LADS AND GANGS

A HOT COMMODITY - OFFERED FOR FREE

Employment pools like this are potentially hot commodities. Elsewhere in the industry, construction workers routinely pay recruiters in the region of £20 a month to be on their books – a similar fee to some traditional union memberships.

The moderators of Lads and Gangs have been approached by recruiters and marketing companies, who either want to collaborate or buy them out. "None of the companies seem to benefit the group, you know. It's okay to say 'it'd be safe to work with a recruitment company', but then it might only be their jobs that were posted," says Walshe. "All the other companies would have to go through them. I'm not going to do that. It's not what it was for and it won't work. The group would lose its feel."

Walshe doesn't get anything financially from running the group – and still, he's always looking to improve the space for workers. He has considered creating his own website for construction workers, or an official place to get advice, but believes it would be difficult to build a consensus for what that would look like among other moderators. In the meantime Facebook provides a nigh inevitable default.

"If I posted a picture of a perfectly blue sky with a cloud in the middle of it, somebody would say 'that's not a perfect blue sky'. And we start arguing over it. I don't have the time. Or the energy. If it came across, right? If something else was done, then I'd say the word, go for it. But at the moment I don't have the capacity, the energy or the ability to," says Walshe.

THE POTENTIAL FOR UNIONS

Lads and Gangs is an example of how power can be built among workers, on widely used public platforms, who wouldn't necessarily look to an official union. It also shows how a critical mass of people can have immense bargaining power when it comes to setting things such as a standard wage.

These kinds of groups could offer an opportunity for existing trade unions to organise workers in a more official way. If unions were able to get even a fraction of those within these kinds of communities on board, supporting admins with funding and putting more formalised organising infrastructure in place, their power may be immense.

As it stands, Walshe says he feels there is a lack of knowledge among the construction workers that use these groups about what a trade union could do for them. Which may be a great place for unions to start.

[1213]

Link: www.facebook.com/groups/345583499354870

GLASSDOOR

HOW A MILLION-DOLLAR CORPORATION WENT TO COURT
TO PROTECT ANONYMOUS WORKER WHISTLEBLOWER

> **JOE WIGGINS, GLASSDOOR COMMS OFFICER**
> *"It's as simple as that, it really has got to the point now where a bad Glassdoor review could be a deal breaker, and you might not even realise it."*

Glassdoor is the corporate face of workplace organising – a jobs board and review website where employees can post anonymously about their experience of working at any organisation.

It provides details such as salaries offered, what people were asked at interviews and more granular information on what it may be like to work for particular teams. As of mid-2021, more than 95 million reviews and insights were available, on around 1.7 million companies across the world.

It is a two-sided platform, with current and former employees on one hand, and employers on the other. Employers can pay the company to list their jobs, as well as for branded advertising, to promote why their company is a great place to work. The reviews on the site ask employees to list the pros and cons of working

1.0 ★ ☆ ☆ ☆ ☆ ⌄

Former Employee, less than 1 year

Horrible

24 Feb 2022 - Warehouseman

✘ Recommend

— CEO Approval

✘ Business Outlook

Pros
It good for short term work for money

Cons
You work as an animal with 3 breaks which are 15 min long

Be the first to find this review helpful

😊 Helpful   ⤴ Share   ⚑ Report

Screenshot, accessed 29/07/2022, Glassdoor

somewhere. For jobseekers, this can highlight potential red flags before they apply.

One review of a tech giant paints a picture:

> **Pros**
> Cool brand with generous maternity pay and nice offices (when open).
>
> **Cons**
> Toxic culture – reports of fear/blame management across many teams.
> Reported bullying not taken seriously. One guy lied over and over again about his team's performance and his own actions and got away with it.
> Poor feedback systems and performance reviews were a joke. Compensation was terrible.

Another reviewer of a media brand writes:

> **Pros**
> Fun (relatively young) colleagues
> Plenty of opportunities to diversity skillset
> Some in-house training provided
>
> **Cons**
> Bad salary
> Sales team got most of the benefits
> Difficult to progress unless someone leaves

People use it to talk about everything from harassment to racism – and while all sorts of things could come out in a review – Glassdoor has specific guidelines about what people can and can't say. Posters are banned from talking about sensitive company information and revealing the names of individuals below the c-suite, or who aren't public facing. Wiggins says that any organisation that has consistently poor reviews, over time and on similar themes, can find it very difficult to recruit.

"It really has got to the point now where a bad Glassdoor review could be a deal breaker, and you might not even realise it. Companies might not even realise, because people aren't even in their pipeline, they're not even bothering to apply, as opposed to applying and then dropping out."

LABOUR MARKET DATA

Glassdoor also has a research team working behind the scenes, with a chief economist and a team of data scientists producing reports for corporate clients on labour metrics, such as gender and ethnicity pay gaps. In short, it holds a lot of useful, precise and anonymous data about work and conditions.

"I don't think there's any one organisation that has the same breadth of data on offer," says Wiggins, corporate comms officer at Glassdoor. "Certainly not on a global scale. And it's really the scale that is important here, because the opinion of two, three or four people is useful, but the opinion of 30, 40, 50, 100-plus people starts to give you a really good trend."

Glassdoor also helps outsiders piece together the value of companies from a variety of different angles. MIT produces a culture index[18] each year using Glassdoor data, looking at values such as diversity, respect, integrity and innovation to try to measure how good a place may be to work. The index is widely covered by the press and the findings are known to influence top-level decision-makers.

Investment banks and analysts use Glassdoor data from an environmental, social and governance (ESG) point of view. When writing investment notes on sectors or certain companies, they heavily reference the platform as a way of understanding how an organisation works. Investors, shareholders and venture capitalists may use it as a means for valuing a company, which incentivises businesses to avoid bad reviews.

A PLACEHOLDER UNION?

Glassdoor stands as a recognised global brand offering a centralised space for improving people's working lives. Wiggins agrees that it could be seen as a potential placeholder for a union in sectors where there are few official organisers. "I guess unions would typically be bargaining for better conditions and better pay. That's what you can do by leveraging the power of Glassdoor," Wiggins says.

"In terms of pay, it's obvious. The more data points there are on Glassdoor, the more certain you can be about whether it's correct. We indicate alongside any salary on Glassdoor how confident we are in that, depending on the data." Wiggins says he has also seen instances where individuals have used it to make ethical shopping decisions. "From the point of view of a customer using a delivery app, they are asking, 'are you trading that convenience of getting a pint of milk or a loaf of bread within 10 minutes for any detriment on the employee side?'."

Operating a platform like this, being a company with power to flex, doesn't come without pushback. Companies do, from time-to-time, try to find out the identity of people who post damning reviews. Glassdoor has gone to court before, because of issues related to anonymity, in order to protect its users.

"We stand for free speech," says Wiggins. "And if it fills a gap, whereby there is no other way of collectively giving a voice kind of at scale, then data stores are a great kind of backup in the absence of something else." The company is predominantly based in the US and has so far only fought such cases in its own courts. "We heavily support users. I think that speaks to the credibility of the content on site; the fact that you get the good, and the bad, and everything in between."

BIG DATA, BIG MONEY

Ultimately, readily accessible employee reviews can force employers to improve their working environment. If the labour market is competitive, this may raise employee conditions everywhere. The strength of Glassdoor is in its critical mass. Its immense datasets offer ways for people to understand what good work is, where they may find it, and avoid negative working and buying experiences, while institutions can track relevant industrial changes. Such data also brings financial backing and commercial clout. This means it can back its contributors and go to court to protect anonymity when needed.

Given that this giant of workplace accountability exists, it presents the question for unions today – could new relationships be brokered, and data leveraged, to support workplace organising?

Link: www.glassdoor.co.uk

CROWDJUSTICE AND #DONOTPAY

HOW NEW PLATFORMS ARE GIVING WORKERS ACCESS TO JUSTICE

> **THE NATIONAL GALLERY 27 WORKERS**
>
> *"We want to take this opportunity to recognise the crucial role played by our funders in enabling our case to be heard and the positive judgement to be reached."*

Imagine working for an organisation for 45 years without being given any holiday, sick pay, pension or maternity pay, despite having paid taxes through the payroll as employees. Then, imagine having your contract terminated, without, it would appear, any other option.

This was the case for one of 27 National Gallery employees who lost their job at the cultural institution in 2017. The group of artists and lecturers had spent decades working for the gallery, giving daily talks and running workshops. The organisation insisted that they were self-employed, and therefore had no right to any benefits, or a consultation before the termination of their contracts.

It can often be quite daunting to take employers to court through employment tribunals without the support of a recognised union. The costs of legal representation and the time without work can mount up and end up costing anything from several hundred pounds to tens of thousands of pounds, depending on the complexity of the case. Employers can also threaten, often falsely, that if you lose you might be liable for their legal costs too.

Luckily for the 27 gallery workers, their case arose just as legal crowdfunders were becoming a legitimate means for individuals to try to right such wrongs. The number of cases using legal crowdfunding have snowballed over the past two decades, as high legal fees and shrinking legal aid funds have prompted people to start looking for other resources to support their cases.

NO JUSTICE WITHOUT THE CROWD

CrowdJustice, one of the biggest platforms in crowdfunding legal fights, says it has so far helped people raise upwards of £25 million from more than 800,000 backers. Over the past decade, high-profile disputes, from Brexit to COVID, have led the British public to the platform to make their case, as money remains a significant barrier to justice.

Through their campaign, the National Gallery 27 group of workers raised more than £77,000 for their legal fees, enabling them to take one of the world's most popular art museums to court. The group's lawyers highlighted that they worked with regularity, and were paid through the gallery's payroll, taxed at source and required to attend staff training. The claimants said that the gallery had offered just eight permanent contracts when the terminations were announced, on salary and terms that were allegedly significantly reduced, and to which they did not consent.

After an employment tribunal in central London, Judge A. M. Snelson ruled in March 2019 that it was "unsustainable" for the gallery to describe the workers as self-employed. She did not uphold claims of unfair dismissal. This is thought to be the first case in the public sector to address concerns about workers' rights, after a flurry against companies in the 'gig economy'.

In an update following the judgement, the group wrote: "We have now been successful in agreeing [the] settlement, and we want to take this opportunity to recognise the crucial role played by our funders in enabling our case to be heard and the positive judgement to be reached.

"We are indebted to everyone who has taken the time and energy to help us every step of the way: our friends, family, colleagues, Parliamentarians and of course our legal team at Gordon Dadds and Chris Milsom of Cloisters Chambers. It's been a huge team effort and one we shall never forget."

The crowd here was vital, indeed, the case may never have been fought without its backers. The art world rallied. Some supported because they remembered visiting the gallery and knew the workers, while others said they were going through something similar.

"The world of work is changing and there will be many individuals who are unsure of their status and rights," Marie van der Zyl, a member of the claimants' legal team, told the BBC at the time.[19] "This case gives those individuals hope." It is one of many crowdfunded campaigns against employers, which has been taken to tribunal, but remains precedent-setting in the sector.

Someone currently raising funds through CrowdJustice is Ruth Lane, whose husband, Don, died due to an allegedly poor working environment. Don was an insulin-dependent diabetic and a DPD courier. Ruth is crowdfunding because she believes the delivery firm's rigidly enforced working patterns and financial penalties meant Don struggled to attend vital medical appointments – and died as a result.

"I need your help to get justice for Don and all of those people that work in the gig economy under enormous pressure and threat of penalties," she writes on Crowd-

♥ Someone pledged £20
Match their pledge of £20 >

We are going through this ourselves. Good luck!

♥ Sian pledged £300
Match Sian's pledge of £300 >

Proceeds from raffle from our Friday art history class in Cobham today - with everyone's support, sympathy & hope for a just and fair verdict xx

Screenshot, accessed 18/07/2022, Crowdjustice

Justice. "Please contribute now and share this page so I can fund a legal challenge against his employer."

A LEGAL CASE FOR UNIONS

Other projects have emerged that use technology to try to make costly parts of the legal process more accessible. This includes platforms such as DoNotPay, which claimed to be the "world's first robot lawyer" when it was created by a Stanford student in 2015. DoNotPay uses artificial intelligence to help people challenge things like parking tickets, bank charges and nuisance calls. It does this by producing, personalising and then automatically sending standard templates for legal letters which are used to contest straightforward cases. It claims to have solved over 250,000 cases – and users pay a yearly subscription. One subset of its website is dedicated to providing advice and support for people fighting workplace discrimination on the grounds of age, gender, mental health or sexual identity.

"The legal system shouldn't be pay-to-play," the platform's creator Joshua Browder told Bloomberg[20] in 2021 on the news that DoNotPay had raised $10 million (£7.6 million) from venture capitalists, valuing it at $210 million (£160 million). Though debate remains about whether algorithms can truly level our societies, in 2020, the company was given an award by the American Bar Association for its efforts to ensure better access to justice for those who are less able to pay.

While crowdfunding shows there is a collective conscience willing to help people fight legal battles, and robot lawyers can take on limited discrimination cases, both could be criticised for being sticking plasters for systemic problems. Crowdfunder campaigns often rely on heavy media coverage and a strong emotional story to get off the ground. Automatic templates can also often only help in very straightforward cases. Despite this, many who fight cases against their employers will often be too wealthy to qualify for legal aid – yet not wealthy enough to go it alone. Crowdfunders and automation may act as a kind of stand-in for proper legal mechanisms of the state and roles that other institutions should be performing.

This speaks to a widening gap between union-like services and unions themselves. These kinds of mechanisms are being used particularly in industries that aren't covered by traditional forms of worker protection. Unions typically have robust legal teams, who should be exploring how to help fight high-profile cases like the one fought by the workers at the National Gallery.

Link: www.crowdjustice.com

WORKER INFO EXCHANGE

HOW TO FIGHT BACK WHEN YOUR BOSS IS AN ALGORITHM

> **JAMES FARRER, FOUNDER OF WORKER INFO EXCHANGE**
>
> *"It's more than just access to data. It's also the right to an explanation of algorithmic control, or algorithmic management."*

Data ownership has become a crucial battleground in the fight for worker rights, particularly in the gig economy.

One such battle started with James Farrar, now founder and director of Worker Info Exchange, who had begun driving for Uber after he left a job at software company SAP. Just weeks in, he was assaulted while on a job, so he called the ride-hailing company to get help tracking down the person who did it so he could report them to the police. Uber refused to give him the passenger's information, saying this breached data security.

Farrar came up with a plan to try to reclaim his data and understand how it was being used by Uber by doing 'subject access requests' on the company; these are a legal right that allow anyone in the UK to ask any organisation whether they are using or storing their personal information, as well as being able to get copies of that data.

Farrar says he was provided with some of his own data, after what he describes as "multiple and continuous" messages to the company, but there were still gaps. There were years of backlogged GPS data and trip ratings given by passengers, as well as a lack of information about the tags he knew were assigned to his profile.

This lack of transparency, and what appeared to be manipulation of data, led Farrar to take Uber to court for its failure to disclose these records. The thing that concerned Farrar and his legal team was a lack of access to data that should have been readily available. "Uber came to the tribunal with sheets of data on my working profile," says Farrar. "They had given me nothing."

It was already well-known that algorithmic control of workers was embedded in Uber's business model. The company had been exposed for experimenting with techniques from video games and non-cash rewards to incentivise drivers. It was found to have manipulated its workers by experimenting with routes, notifications and more. "It's more than just access to data. It's also the right to an explanation of algorithmic control, or algorithmic management," Farrar says.

To keep drivers working for longer, it had also taken advantage of some people's tendency to set earnings goals – sending a push notification as they tried to clock off if they were close to hitting another target. This inevitably made the job worse – drivers worked longer hours and harder shifts for less money – while Uber reaped the profits.

Farrar's legal case would set a new legal precedent, and led him to help set up the non-profit Worker Info Exchange in 2019, to help other drivers like him. As a result, subject access requests have become a key tool in their fight to understand how the company was controlling their working lives.

POOLING DATA FOR CHANGE

Uber drivers wanted access to information that would help them calculate their minimum wage, clarify their employment status and evidence discrimination. Without it, any collective bargaining for better terms was proving difficult. So drivers started using subject access requests to ask the company for granular data from algorithmic profiles and about how the platform performance manages them. The Worker Info Exchange acted as a 'data trust' – the place for drivers to collect and pool this information.

support of the Worker Info Exchange, 70,000 UK drivers brought a legal case claiming Uber was breaking UK employment law by failing to offer basic workers' rights, such as holiday pay and the national minimum wage. After a six-year battle, in February 2021, the Supreme Court ruled[21] that they must be recognised as workers rather than self-employed contractors. Finally they were guaranteed a minimum wage, pension and holiday pay, as well as safeguards for whistleblowers and protection against discrimination.

The Worker Info Exchange continues the work Farrar and his fellow drivers began with this case. As well as enabling drivers to bring cases in the UK, the trust has made it easier to fight for rights in other jurisdictions, too. All of Uber's data outside of North America is controlled in Amsterdam, meaning Worker Info Exchange is able exercise GDPR rights extraterritorially. Using this power, Worker Info Exchange helped an Australian driver get access to their data. Next, one of the trust's aims is to create an API (an intermediary software that allows two applications to talk to each other) to let drivers share their records automatically with other drivers.

TECHNOLOGY WON'T SAVE US

Though the win was historic, it alone is not enough to protect workers' rights and it was far from a clear-cut victory for drivers. It triggered yet more need for workers to navigate the legal system in the UK, and further afield, and highlighted how Uber was increasingly relying on a third category of worker. This is one that has some traditional employment protections but not others provided to employees.

Its UK drivers still do not have access to sick pay, parental leave, or time off for emergencies, and they have limited protection against unfair dismissal. Minimum wage stipulations also only apply to the time drivers spend picking up or ferrying around passengers – not the time they spend signed into the app looking for work. Studies have shown that – around half of the time Uber drivers spend on the road – they are looking for work.

Since the Supreme Court case though, Uber drivers have hailed yet more victories. In July of the same year, the workers' won recognition for their trade union, GMB. This has again opened the door to the possibility of further legal action to see workers recognised as employees. This would also make the company liable for national insurance contributions.

Data stewardship models like data trusts, which bring

workers and their data together, show how the gig economy, and the platforms controlling this labour, have complicated digital rights issues at their core. It also points to how important it is to ensure people can understand, or be protected from the harms that technology can cause, and how complicated it can be to get control over your own data.

This becomes all the more important as digital and AI legislation evolve, and how these incorporate or interact with employment law. Uber is the case study, but algorithmic control is endemic in how platforms operate across the world. Use of algorithms means companies can often stay a step ahead of regulators, confusing officials and disguising the exploitation that unions have worked hard to stamp out. Here, workers clawed back some of their rights and gained bargaining power by taking collective control of their data – and unions should be keen to learn from this.

LINK: www.workerinfoexchange.org

#PUBLISHINGPAIDME

HOW HASHTAG ACTIVISM CHANGED THE TIDE ON
INDUSTRY DISCRIMINATION

> LL MCKINNEY, AUTHOR AND CREATOR OF
> #PUBLISHINGPAIDME
>
> *"We're here because publishing, like so many of these other industries and companies, only has something to say when shit pops off."*

What would a book on modern organising be without a story about a viral hashtag?

The social media campaign #PublishingPaidMe brought to light the stories that publishers value – those they are willing to stump up cash for – by calling for pay transparency. It particularly highlighted the disparities between what white and Black authors are awarded, and – to some extent – the inherent bias in whose stories the industry chooses to tell.

#PublishingPaidMe originated in the summer of 2020, following an outpouring of grief online in response to the death of George Floyd, a Black man, at the hands of a white police officer. A dam burst online as demands that #BlackLivesMatter flooded platforms – giving space for some frank conversations about racial inequalities.

A DAM BURSTING

It was in this moment that US-based author LL McKinney, a Black woman, called on others in the industry to share what they were paid as an advance. These are the part-payments typically awarded to authors when a book contract is signed.

She said she started the hashtag without a plan, but had been mulling the responses to a tweet by fellow Black young adult (YA) fiction author Tochi Onyebuchi. Onyebuchi had called for white authors to publicly declare their advances in order to foster industry solidarity and transparency, tweeting:

> *"You've got to get ready to have some real uncomfortable convos about how much you've been paid for your books"*

Many replied, saying they would disclose what they were paid.

In since deleted Tweets, on June 6 2020 McKinney, wrote:

> *"Do y'all need a hashtag? #PublishingPaidMe There you go."*

Speaking to the American news website Vox,[22] McKinney said: "We expected there to be disparities. We did not expect them to be as wide as they were."

What followed was an outpouring from the publishing community, as people from all sides shared their rates. Best-selling authors such as Matt Haig, who wrote *Reasons to Stay Alive* and *The Midnight Library*, and Roxane Gay, known for *Bad Feminist: Essays and Hunger*, were moved to disclose their advances, among thousands of others.

At the time, Haig, who is white and British, called it "seriously uncomfy", but said he was paid £5,000 as an advance for his first title. He had steadily earned more since. His 10th book netted him an advance of £600,000.

Black American author Gay said that she received a $12,500 (£9,562) advance for *An Untamed State*, $15,000 (£11,474) for *Bad Feminist*, $100,000 (£76,497) for Hunger, $150,000 (£114,742) for *The Year I Learned*

Everything and "a significant jump" for her next two non-fiction books.

"Keep your day job," she said on Twitter, calling publishers' statements about diversity "nonsense".

"A little Instagram post doesn't make up for racial disparities in everything else," she added.

NON-DISCLOSURE AGREEMENTS

Meanwhile, former childrens' laureate Malorie Blackman, who is Black and British, said she could not disclose her pay due to the fact she had signed a non-disclosure agreement. But she tweeted that she was paid "NOWHERE near what some white authors are getting for their nth book where n is a single digit."

This sharing of information prompted the creation of a crowdsourced Google spreadsheet, which is still available as of summer 2022 today,[23] under The Transparency Project, started by Onyebuchi to use the data to hold publishers to account. They pledged to give $2 per submission to the sheet to #BLM organisations.

The sheet splits the information into book genre, amount paid in US dollars, the kind of distribution rights signed, year of sale, the name of the publishing house, whether it was a first book and whether the author had an agent. Also gathered was people's race, gender identity, sexual orientation and whether or not the author has a disability.

Authors could give their name when disclosing, add their book titles and any additional comments. The form received more than 2,800 responses and is the most comprehensive, open database of publishing-industry data today. The data reveals that, while some academic writers receive nothing for writing books, others had netted advances of up to $2.5 million (£1.9 million).

Some of the lack of transparency here can be put down to corporate gagging rules, as many major publishers have company policies that prevent authors discussing advances, even among themselves. While the campaign gained support in many areas, some in the industry pointed out that the sheet only included a narrow sample, and that an advance is only one part of a publishing deal.

Others expressed shock at the fact that some early advances for now-famous Black authors were comparatively small compared to their white counterparts. They also highlighted how few authors of colour had received big advances for their debuts. McKinney's conclusion from the episode was that "publishing literally does not value black voices".

"When books by white authors don't perform, they're likely to get another chance and another 100k advance. When books by black authors don't perform, the ENTIRE demographic gets blamed and punished. Black authors are told our books don't sell. No one wants them," she tweeted at the time.

"We're here because publishing, like so many of these other industries and companies, only has something to say when shit pops off," McKinney added, pointing to "the performative posts from publishers we've seen following protests and the loss of black life".

Two big publishers – Hachette and Penguin Random House – subsequently committed to publishing their own audits, which they said would look at the number of titles they publish by people of colour. These decisions followed walkouts, where employees sought to force their employers to address racism within their organisations.

Hachette's report, published in May 2021,[24] showed that 71% of book contracts it signed in 2020 were with white authors. As such, the publisher committed to raising its starting salaries in the US and began a recruitment drive to attract more candidates of colour.

Penguin's audit, published in December 2021,[25] showed that 74.9% of the authors of books it published in the US between January 2019 and the end of 2021 were white. The company concluded that it would work to integrate demographic data collection into its normal business practices, including a questionnaire when onboarding contributors.

"We are not in the place we would like to be," the report said. "Since the acquisitions take place at the divisional level, the heart of this work lies with our publishers. Each division has committed to deeply exploring their specific systemic barriers and then identifying and implementing solutions tailored to their audit results and set of findings."

It remains to be seen whether this action will force a long-term, material change within the publishing industry. It did, however, show that strength in numbers – both people and figures – and putting easily accessible tools to work in the open, plus the embarrassment factor, can all be useful for bargaining with powerful, legacy industries.

An online moment allowed people who felt their voices were literally worth less to speak up, then work together to draw meaningful comparisons and mobilise against those holding power. The database is now a piece of publishing history – something that would be difficult to replicate given the catalyst of the #BlackLivesMatter movement, and the initial bravery of those who had experienced injustice.

The work of McKinney and others has set the foundation for how community data collection can be used as a tactic for highlighting injustices in pay and building solidarity. Unions would do well to expand these methods to other closed traditional industries to strengthen workers' negotiating power and help foster inclusivity.

Link: docs.google.com/spreadsheets/d/1Xsx6rKJta-fa8f_prlYYD3zRxaXYVDaPXbasvt_iA2vA

SPOONSTRIKE

HOW A GROUP CHAT TOOK ON A PUB GIANT

> **TRADES UNION CONGRESS (TUC)**
>
> *"It was the start of a really fruitful, long-term conversation that was going on between people who could never normally meet, talking about the challenges of working in that environment."*

Pantomime villain Wetherspoons boss Tim Martin has never been one to stay quiet in times of national crisis. So, as the UK was catapulted into its first lockdown in 2020, it was no surprise when he appeared via video link, pint in hand, with a message.

He'd previously told his staff they would be subject to regular statutory sick-pay rules if they were forced to self-isolate due to COVID, even before the first lockdowns had kicked in. At the time, the Trades Union Congress (TUC) estimated that nearly two million UK workers were not earning enough to qualify for statutory sick pay, including one in 10 working women – a measure which would become crucial for many as hospitality started to open up again as lockdowns eased in June 2020.

This time, the news was worse. The message he had for the 43,000 workers was that, as the UK was all but shut, he would not be waiting for government support to kick in before sending them home. Martin said he would simply close the pubs and stop paying his workers, many of whom were on contracts. The business couldn't afford the outlay, he said.

As the reality of this set in, the finer details of the furlough scheme were still a glint in the Treasury's eye, but COVID was not going away. As a stop gap, Martin said workers should seek employment in Tesco, which was hiring staff to meet increased demand for food delivery and distribution. Some in the public eye quickly came to the workers' defence.

At the time, Rachel Reeves MP, the chair of the business select committee, said the decision was unacceptable, pointing out that companies may not receive government support until late April, leaving staff out of pocket until then. Ian Hodson, the president of the Bakers and Allied Food Workers Union (BAFWU), also called on the business to change its plan, saying the actions were "shocking".

"He is ignoring the advice of the government to stand by your workers and instead abandoning them in their time of need," he said. "They need to pay rent, buy food and because of the low wages he's always paid them, will not have savings to depend upon. His selfish approach says unless the government puts money into my bank account today he'll let the workers who have made him rich suffer. It is completely unacceptable."

But, behind the scenes, a movement was kicking into gear.

IT STARTED WITH A GROUP CHAT

While some unions have been slow to use new technology within their networks, the BFAWU and the TUC had a plan. It started with a select number of pubs, which the BFAWU already had a presence in, and quickly spread nationwide.

First, workers began to gather information from employees through an online form, collecting their experiences about the reality of what was happening on the ground. Then, as word spread about the campaign, 250 workers were brought together into WhatsApp groups. An organised 'happy hour' each evening – a time slot where people could air their grievances – meant people's phones were not flooded with messages at all hours of the day.

This was a way of seeing what was going on across different pubs and remotely joining the dots between the many branches. A statement from the BFAWU and

SpoonStrike, a group of the affected employees, led to a petition which gained more than 12,000 signatures, as well as a letter signed by 80 MPs. Soon Martin backtracked, and committed to continuing weekly payments to his staff while furlough plans were drawn up. But this wasn't the end of the fight.

SpoonStrike continued to put pressure on the business as the end of the various lockdown periods approached, collating a list of back-to-work demands and getting their message out via Twitter. These included what might be considered basic safety requirements, such as readily available personal protective equipment, cashless tills and full sick pay from day one. Workers also recorded videos voicing concerns about the working conditions as the economy opened up again, which were used as campaign materials.

LONG-TERM CONVERSATIONS AND SUSTAINABLE CHANGE?

"It was the start of a really fruitful, long-term conversation that was going on between people who could never normally meet, talking about the challenges of working in that environment," says John Wood, digital manager at the TUC.

By writing an organising code for Wetherspoons – a guide which others could follow – and working with other organisers within BFAWU, crucial alliances were made with other parts of the industry, and worker voices were heard for what felt like the first time.

"They got people willing to step up and talk about how working at Wetherspoons was affecting them and give some really good personal testimony," says Wood. He thinks things are slowly changing in unions, with a shift to digital partially accelerated because of the pandemic.

Despite this encouraging progress, many unions are still slow to make the most of digital tools for organising. The generational lag in membership means unions more broadly have been slower to adapt and experiment, a key challenge which they will need to overcome.

FUCK YOU, PAY ME

HOW INSTAGRAM INFLUENCERS ARE STANDING UP FOR CREATORS

> **LINDSEY LEE LUGRIN, CEO OF FYPM**
>
> *"There's never been a baseline, or a place where you can safely discuss creator pay besides your own inner circle. And then even so, that conversation feels invasive sometimes."*

Some movements to combat poor or unfair working conditions start with a clear moment, like #PublishingPaidMe, while others are catalysed by a pent-up collection of injustices over time. The platform Fuck You, Pay Me (FYPM) is one such example of the latter.

The California-based company is working to make the labour market a fairer place for 'creators' – people who make money by creating content for social-media platforms such as Instagram.

It s itself as a kind of 'GlassDoor for social-media influencers'.

Aptly named, it was originally one woman's "ode to frustration brought about by unfair pay". "There's never been a baseline, or a place where you can safely discuss creator pay besides your own inner circle. And then even so that conversation feels invasive sometimes," says co-creator Lindsey Lee Lugrin.

FYPM is working to plug this information gap in the million-dollar global influencing industry by hosting a crowdsourced database of this kind of information. Users can submit what they have been paid for different branded campaigns, as well as details about themselves, including their follower count.

The goal is to give online creators a way to understand whether they are being paid fairly, and a reference point before they enter into a new contract with a new client. This is a space where traditional unions, no doubt, have a blind spot.

INFLUENCE FOR FREE

LA-based model Lugrin's career began when she won a competition on the Facebook-owned photo-sharing platform Instagram. This resulted in her face being plastered on boards and appearing in magazines for global fashion brand Marc Jacobs. At the time, she was delighted, but for the pleasure, she was only paid

$1,000 – a miniscule cost for a fashion brand with millions in the bank – for a campaign that was getting global exposure.

Frustrated with modelling, Lugrin went to work in finance, where she built a following by creating satirical content about sexism in the workplace through the @MsYoungProfessional handle on Instagram and a blog. As she pulled long hours making original content and building a following, her engagement figures grew fast, leading brands contact her for endorsements.

"Again, nobody wanted to pay me," said Lugrin. "I lived and breathed this problem in several different areas of my life." Over years in the industry, her frustration lack of bargaining power, that she and other content creators had, grew.

There was no open and transparent place for influencers to see what others are paid, and there is still no union that captures the complexities and power dynamics of working in this part of the online economy. According to the Digital Marketing Institute, the influencer-marketing industry is expected to hit $13.8 ion (£10.6 ion) in value by 2022,[26] surpassing traditional print advertising by some margin.

Lugrin found growing, publicly unvoiced concerns among other influencers about what seemed to be increasing disparities with how much people were paid in the industry. Data has since backed this up. In 2020, influencer-marketing platform Klear polled more than 4,800 creators and found male creators were paid $476 on average per post, while women made just $348.[27]

After years of thinking about how she could make a change, Lugrin and her co-creator Isha Mehra, 25, a former Facebook data scientist, launched F*** You Pay Me. By July 2021, the app was up, running and distributed to a small number of testers.

To get access, users have to verify their identity and share a review of a brand they have worked with. In its first months, the pair had approved 1,500 people and rejected almost 1,200. FYPM had also already received almost 2,000 reviews – including clothing companies, ranging from fast fashion to luxury, beauty brands and even political parties.

Because the platform was first launched around the time of the United States' presidential election, there's data on the amounts people were paid here by political parties. There's also a review of Yorkshire's Kirklees Council in the UK, which paid an influencer to promote the coronavirus vaccine.

The platform quickly drew significant press attention – in August, the *New York Times* splashed headline "The App Unprintable Name That Wants to Give Power to Creators" across its front page. *The Observer* also profiled the app and Lugrin in September 2021.[28]

SHIFTING THE INFLUENCER-BRAND POWER DYNAMIC

Lugrin says that what's at the heart of the platform is a twisted power dynamic between influencers and brands. Influencers are usually one-person shows – often shooting, editing and promoting all of their own content, usually across multiple platforms.

Most do so without an agent, and there are no standard rates for what it costs an individual like this to produce an image or video as part of an advertising campaign. Fees are often casually negotiated through emails or direct messages on social-media platforms. Despite its huge and growing economic value, influencing remains an industry that isn't always taken as seriously as other creative professions. "Influencing is not seen as a real job. But it really is. And I think a lot of that has to do with sexism and what we value as a society," says Lugrin.

FYPM sits among a number of more unofficial collaborations that are attempting to help creators understand what their work is worth. Groups on social media such as We Don't Work For Free, Influencer Pay Gap and Brands Behaving Badly have come some way in achieving this. Online communities such as Creative Girl Gang have also allowed influencers to lift the curtain on their experiences with different companies.

FYPM is trying to create an official place where creators can call out exploitation, providing the tools and data that may help people argue better for fair pay. As it grows, Lugrin wants to keep the platform free for influencers. She says that in the past, similar businesses in the space have tried to charge, or take a cut of what creators earn.

The goal for FYPM is tend its remit to all gig economy workers, including freelance writers and filmmakers. "I really want this thing to help people. I have three degrees, and I'm really fucking smart, and I have never been financially independent. This to me is key to unleashing that for so many people all over the world," says Lugrin.

NEW WORK COMES FASTER THAN NEW RIGHTS

The value of this market, and the interest in FYPM, shows that these new forms of value-creating work have appeared faster than the workers' rights necessary to protect people. Holding companies to account isn't easy at the best of times, but what influencers do have is influence, which can only grow with a critical mass.

The creation of this, and other GlassDoor-esque platforms, has to be a way of taking control of some of the mill ions of dollars that don't seem to be flowing to the people doing the work. It is also a way of gathering the necessary data to try to bridge age-old inequalities, such as gender and ethnicity pay gaps.

As a platform created by someone in the industry, it has come from the needs of workers, people who are not being protected by traditional unions. New ways of organising may need to be built specifically by workers, for their needs, rather than bending current systems to fit new problems.

Link: www.fypm.vip

ORGANISE

A NEW PLATFORM FOR WORKERS TO TAKE ACTION TOGETHER

> NAT WHALLEY, ORGANISE CEO
>
> *"There's something in this idea of connecting people to take collective action super rapidly in the moments of pain."*

The UK's McDonald's employees had a complaint to make – they kept burning themselves at work. In fact, thousands of workers across the country were sharing experiences of unsafe equipment, bullying, and a lack of adequate training – through a survey conducted via the Organise platform. One explained:

> *"I wasn't told how to properly clean down the top platens on grills. A huge blob of hot oil dripped onto my hand and ran down my skin. I watched my skin burning off and couldn't run it under water until about 20 minutes later after a sudden busy period. Afterwards I had a huge 'ping pong ball' sized blister and am now left permanently scarred down my hand."*

This anecdote, the stuff of nightmares for most people, was distressingly similar to other stories about severe injuries, and as people spoke out, patterns were identified. Many of these incidents aren't reported to McDonald's management, for fear that managers may cut workers' hours if they complain.

Organise is a campaigning organisation that provides tools, a network and the collective confidence to highlight such workplace issues and to support people to make change happen at work. Founded by campaigners Bex Hay and Nat Whalley, this network-driven platform has the ethos that "better work is possible", and they believe that there is power in numbers.

"It's really hard to know how other people are feeling at work and to do anything about it," says Whalley, CEO. "So we try to create things that help people fix that. The first thing is the tools, things like petitions, open letter calls and surveys that people can easily see on our website."

Organise offers a space for workers to have honest conversations about the problems they are facing without the risk that it gets back to management. It is aimed at bringing together people that are more disconnected from their colleagues than they would have been in the past, particularly because of new forms of digital-powered work.

Today, it may be that you can't just go to the pub and have a chat, because you work miles away from colleagues. It helps people identify common issues and connects those with similar experiences, like workers at fashion-retailer River Island, where people felt they were forced to lie about being sick in order for them to swap shifts so they could attend essential appointments.

One of the social enterprise's most high-profile recent campaigns took on Amazon's returns policy. Under this policy, when customers returned expensive items like TVs they were destroyed - a practice that was seen as demoralising by workers.

So the workers used Organise to connect with people in different warehouses, and through a country-wide survey they were able to generate data on this issue which they took to the press. This forced Amazon to investigate and ban this behaviour in the UK.

As of November 2021, Organise has around 1.4 million registered users, seeing a significant uptick during the COVID-19 pandemic.

FROM ACTIVISTS TO FOUNDERS

Whalley says that if Organise were a superhero, its 'origin story' came when a pregnant friend was fired from their job. The same thing had happened to Whalley's mother 30 years before.

"My friend had no power to challenge it," says Whalley. "And she went to her union and they were like, 'that's kind of how work is'." Seemingly, nothing had changed for pregnant women at work since the 1980s. Legally, the workplace was covered, even if the firing had been morally wrong.

Spurred on by this sense of injustice, a group of friends got together to run a Crowdfunder, to pay for her legal fees to take her employers to court and ultimately see her reinstated. "There's something in this idea of connecting people to take collective action super rapidly in the moments of pain," says Whalley. Because of the noise created by the campaign, she had her job back within 24 hours, and six-months' maternity pay.

Whalley and Hay were both working in digital advocacy before they founded Organise. The pair met at activism non-profit 38 Degrees. Hay had also co-founded Amazon Anonymous, which in 2013 prompted hundreds of thousands of people to boycott the tech giant.

"We knew some of the tools we could use to leverage large groups of people to make change," says Whalley. "And so we started thinking about how you can adapt those tools to make it safe to do work with campaigning online."

The difference between a petition on Organise, as opposed to through the UK Parliament website, for example, is that Organise collects the user's employment status and workplace or industry. This allows them to build networks of people organising in similar areas.

"Hopefully, by talking to each other, finding their shared experiences or their shared pain points, and coming up with ideas on ways to fix it, they find the confidence to take that change forward, and lobby and campaign for change at work," says Whalley.

UNION ADJACENT NOT A REPLACEMENT

Organise has worked on projects with organisations such as Unite, GMB and the Legal Sector Workers United (LSWU). Its campaign LSWU has brought together workers across the legal sector to find the problems with pay across private practice, chambers and law centres through a survey.[29]

A common misconception about Organise is that it is trying to challenge or replace trade unions. "I think unions were quite sceptical seeing us in this space. They were like, 'why are you doing this? What's your motivation?'." The Organise team sees it as a means to give people a tool to find collective power – but they ultimately encourage people to join a union, to ensure long-term representation.

"We're, as a team, deeply passionate about using technology to empower worker voice in collective bargaining. Organise is not a union, nor are we trying to be one," the group says on its website. "The workers pay for and protect this online space for themselves," says Whalley.

"I think the beautiful thing about the power of having a network driven product, is the more people use it, the more valuable it becomes, the more change you can win," says Whalley. "The more people who come and use it kind of compounds itself."

This phenomenon is commonly known as the network effect – an economic theory that describes demand-side economies of scale. As with many of the initiatives chronicled in this book, demand for the platform increased hugely in the pandemic.

"COVID was obviously a massive disruption into people's working lives. And the way they dealt with that is coming online and sharing their experiences and then lobbying for change for different places."

Even without Organise, people are finding ways to connect – some of that is through WhatsApp, or through Facebook groups, however, she says, both of those have their own problems. Whalley says she thinks Organise has taken off, in part, because there aren't currently many spaces online where workers can communicate without the risk of surveillance

"I think it's really important to create protected spaces where you can have those conversations that can't necessarily always be physical anymore. Particularly where the pandemic is concerned – we have heard really creepy reports that bosses are watching you through webcams, or monitoring your mouse movements to check you are working. We want to help combat this."

While Organise has the potential to act as a membership pipeline for Trade Unions, there is a natural tension between the campaigning tone of the new platform and more traditional institutional practices. Not all worker organising can be run as a campaign, as many issues require long term and complex negotiations which might be less easy to attract support for. As new forms of worker organising encounter older institutional methods this is likely to be an emerging tension.

Link: organise.network

WECLOCK

HOW NEW TECHNOLOGY IS TACKLING THE MULTI-ION DOLLAR 'WAGE THEFT' PROBLEM

> JONNIE PENN, ACADEMIC AND WECLOCK CO-CREATOR
>
> *"It was about the means, as well as the ends – that rather than thinking that tech was going to be a silver bullet that would solve everything – we thought, 'what could we do to automate some of the work that organisers already do?'"*

WeClock is an app designed to end the phenomenon of 'wage theft' – where employees are denied wages or benefits that they are rightly owed.

This can range from failure to pay overtime or tips, violation of minimum-wage laws or working 'off the clock', to more subtle problems, such as failure to recognise bad conditions, which can lead to burnout. "Wage theft is a multi-ion dollar crime," says Dr Jonnie Penn, an academic at the University of Cambridge and one of the app's co-creators. "People are not paid for the amount of work they do, in all sorts of different sectors."

According to research from the Economic Policy Institute in 2017, in the 10 most populous US states, 2.4 million workers lose $8 ion (£6.1 ion) every year because of minimum-wage violations.[30] That's an average of $3,300 each for year-round workers – or almost a quarter of their wages. This form of wage theft affects 17% of low-wage workers, with people of all demographics being cheated out of pay.

Perversely, such minimum-wage violations, by definition, affect the lowest-paid workers – those who can least afford to lose out. This loss of earnings causes many families to fall below the poverty line, and this increases workers' reliance on public assistance, costing taxpayers money. Lost wages can hurt local economies. It also harms other workers in affected industries, by putting a downward pressure on wages.

The problem is less acute, but still prevalent in the UK. In 2017, Middlesex University and Trust for London found that at least 2 million workers in the UK were losing around £3 ion a year of unpaid holiday pay and wages – strategies being used by employers to bolster their profits.[31]

PUTTING THE POWER OF THE CLOCK IN PEOPLE'S HANDS

Clocking in and clocking out has been a means for

measuring working hours for more than a century – and WeClock aims to put that power, and data, in the hands of employees. Through the app, people can quantify how much of their time, and wellbeing, is spent at work, and evaluate what is going unchecked, in terms of both pay and conditions.

It moves to counter the rise of surveillance capitalism at work, as increasing numbers of employers try to track employees. The team behind the platform says it can be adopted by all workers to track things such as missed breaks, long commutes, mistreatment, burnout and an inability to disconnect – issues that have plagued the modern workforce amid the rise of the gig economy.

"Allowing people to measure their own working time, the same way they measure their step count, gym time, sleep or anything like that is one solution to this issue," says Penn. He notes that the legal community says the information that WeClock tracks is necessary to push back on wage theft. Unions have told the WeClock team that having more convenient ways to record these different things will give workers more power.

TRACKING YOUR DATA FOR GOOD

The idea was born when technologist Nathan Freitas realised that the tools he was using to help empower journalists and activists could be applied to the labour market. Freitas had been working Guardian Project, a global collective of developers, designers, advocates, activists and trainers who develop open-source mobile-security software and try to improve digital operating systems.

With the core principle of tracking your data 'for good', Freitas, Christina J. Colclough and Penn set out to experiment with new methods to help workers take their data into their own hands. Penn and Freitas had set up the Young Workers Lab at UNI Global Union, which represents about 20 million workers around the globe in hundreds of different organisations.

"We were thinking independently about the appropriate intervention, given where platform work is going, and the kind of hopelessness that there is among so many young people," Penn says.

"It started with a pretty wild and big vision," adds Freitas. "Like, what if we could intercept all of the data Uber holds and copy it? We were thinking about the asymmetry in data between what the employers have, versus what the workers actually get. From the start we were not supposed to produce a polished brand and app."

Penn, a historian of technology, says the aim was to drop the myth that our lives will be fully automated through technology, and start to build structures that support people better than privately held and monopolised infrastructure. "So it was about the means, as well as the ends – that rather than thinking that tech was going to be a silver bullet that would solve everything – we thought, 'what could we do to automate some of the work that organisers already do?'," says Penn.

"One vision was that we were creating an open-source framework or toolkit that any union could adopt," adds Freitas.

COLLABORATIVE, ONGOING PRODUCT DEVELOPMENT

When it came to building the product, what it boiled down to was helping people collate and track data about their workplace. WeClock works with ACV, a union in the Netherlands and Belgium, which contributed a small grant to the project.

Prior to this, ACV had already looked at existing, proprietary time-tracking features and apps, but didn't want to tie their members into these platforms, because they simply didn't trust them. The union requested features such as manual time tracking and to localise the app for Dutch workers. And the WeClock team is now teaching them how to work data.

Every time a new group uses the app, the team aims to develop it further for that need. "It's a community effort, through an open-source project as well," says Freitas. The project has tended to focus on quality of life measures, for example, length and frequency of breaks, or whether a worker is sitting versus standing. Through the Apple Watch version, it can monitor a worker's heart rate. Though this sounds scary, data on heart rate can be used to measure stress which may be useful evidence if a union is trying to prove that a company has a bad culture of workplace bullying or overwork.

Another aspect the team has looked at, particularly during the COVID-19 pandemic, has been finding a practical application for precise location data, for example, to chart where employees might be in a warehouse, which produces heat maps. "We're still in the stage of looking at how to put that all together into a specific kind of campaign or movement that the unions can understand," says Freitas.

The team feels that WeClock partially addresses the need for unions to work to serve a younger demographic. "Unions are, in our experience, designed to serve older people. So it's older people voting on behalf of their cohort, not necessarily voting for their children or people that age," says Penn.

But the WeClock team see the app as a way to help trade unions, to arm them with data, while freeing up time they may have spent collecting it, not simply automating the work they do. WeClock's aim is also for vulnerable communities to be able to make and own their own infrastructure.

DIGITAL TOOLS, NOT DIGITAL LIVES

Yet, the team does not want to normalise the fact that many aspects of people's working life have gone digital. The solution to this issue is not simply having a union go digital too.

"The transition to digital hollows out some of the integrity and sovereignty of different institutions," says Penn. "Being on the receiving end of an API and getting your work through Uber, or another delivery platform, whatever it is, things get lost. You don't have co-workers you see regularly or a manager you can challenge when things go wrong. In this respect, the future world of work is pretty shitty, actually.

"We want to draw attention to some of these tensions and problems and remind folks that there are other ways of doing this, and that governments still have room to act to prevent the worst of it."

Beyond WeClock's current form, the team wants to figure out new ways for people to join campaigns and collectivise their data, Freitas explains. This function will help people find out where they stand with other people, as well as making it easier to contribute more widely.

THE WATCHERS BECOME THE WATCHED

Legally, it's not enough to merely feel like you are being exploited – you have to be able to show it. WeClock shows that this is partly about who owns the data and infrastructure for work – and a dangerous precedent has been set, where much of our personal information is held on and managed through private, monopolised infrastructure.

Much of what tech has done for work over the past decade has meant it has become more fragmented and less personal too – and so the solution is not simply that all unions or organisations advocating for workers should switch to a totally digital product.

The WeClock team hopes to build collective power relationally and through technology, while understanding that people are central to the product, and that tech cannot solve all ills alone. This represents an interesting moment for surveillance capitalism – as more metrics are measured by workers themselves – the watchers may become the watched.

Link: weclock.it

THE GRAPEVINE

HOW TV AND FILM WORKERS BOOTSTRAPPED A UNION

> PAUL EVANS, RESEARCH OFFICER AT THE BROADCASTING, ENTERTAINMENT, COMMUNICATIONS AND THEATRE UNION (BECTU)
>
> *"I don't want you to join a union, I don't think that really makes sense. I want you to form a union."*

"The first rule of the grapevine is not to talk about the grapevine," jokes Paul Evans, research officer at BECTU.

Evans is alluding to a quiet network of WhatsApp groups that helps regulate pay and conditions in the entertainment sector. There are different groups for those working as on-set electricians, for example, and on other parts of production.

People on 'the grapevine' use the network to consult with each other and negotiate their rates in real-time. It is an informal, digital infrastructure – that enables the subsets of freelancers who make the TV and film industries tick – to effectively design their own rate cards.

"The freelancers that BECTU helps tend to be a lot less deferential than full-time employees. They tend to want stuff to happen straight away. They don't give themselves up to a lot of the structured approaches that other unions take," says Evans. "The idea that you have to wait until the meeting, and then you have to raise it as a point of order and all that, they're really not really keen on any of that. They're problem solvers."

So, when one worker is offered a job at a certain rate, before accepting, they will go to their sector-specific group – which contains many of the only workers in the country trained to do that job – to consult on whether they have been offered a fair rate. They have instant wage information and negotiating power at their fingertips, as people weigh in on what they think that job is worth.

They get both strength in numbers and a kind of industry consensus among employees in negotiation with employers. Evans says that in some circumstances, when negotiating a contract, a worker could have 80 opinions on the rate offered by an employer within 10 minutes. If a rate that is offered remains below the consensus, people in the group agree not to take the job.

Evans says that BECTU members are very good at using, adapting and bootstrapping existing technologies. "So when WhatsApp groups came along, they were on it straight away. You know, it's encrypted, it's all private, they could control who's in it."

The grapevine is behavioural economics in action. It encourages the supply-side to withhold labour until favourable conditions are reached for individuals, thus pushing up standards for everyone else.

Evans feels the solidarity brought by being in groups such as these should be core principles of union organising. "I don't just say to people: 'Look, we're not gonna do anything for you. That's not what we're for'. I say: 'I don't want you to join a union. I want you to form a union.'"

'DRIVE BY' CONSULTATION

Typically these groups are run separately from central BECTU activity and don't include union officials. However, those within the network work as a group to report back any concerns to the union as they arise.

In turn, organisers can use this existing tech to reach out to those in their network to get opinions on any issues facing the industry. "I call it drive-by consultation, where you have to get people to tell you what they think or what their concerns are as quickly as possible. You have to do it in a way that doesn't doesn't exhaust them and doesn't bore them, but you get the information out of them," says Evans.

"And then you find a way of agreeing on a description of the problem and getting them signed up to it, then you need to agree to a description of the solution, you have to agree what it is you want."

Since the pandemic hit, Evans has also been using Zoom and Microsoft Teams meetings with screen-sharing, to help members work together to define the main problems they have been facing. This technology hadn't been readily accepted en masse in BECTU (or many other workplaces) before lockdowns.

With the entertainment industry all but shut for much of 2020, there were many justified anxieties: fears about when the industry would open up again, safety, pay, support schemes for freelancers, and how those on PAYE contracts - who had not been furloughed - would cope.

During these calls, instead of a shared document where many people can collaboratively edit at once, such as a Google Doc, Evans worked as the sole editor. "We just discovered [that way of doing things] spontaneously by me putting a Microsoft Word document on the screen and then sharing my screen," he says. He incorporated the concerns of the group until they came to an agreement on what the core issue actually was and what they wanted to get out of taking action.

Through this method, BECTU were able to compile six sets of detailed documents on the big issues facing the sector at the start of the pandemic – documents they were still using in December 2021. As lockdowns dragged on, this method enabled rolling consultations industry and meant BECTU could create an action plan for how the sector could work, and respond quickly, in a COVID-safe way.

"There is something really important, I think, in letting people see their own hands in the policy that has been applied to them," says Evans. The resulting document amounted to around 100 pages that helped to reassure insurance companies that the industry could operate safely.

It had an economic impact greater than the sum of its parts, showing that reopening the entertainment industry could happen even in the midst of a pandemic. "We were able to give the industry something that really did help them open the industry a lot earlier," he adds.

BECTU's use of existing technologies, and support for the everyday approaches favoured by workers, shows how solutions don't have to be costly or centrally controlled. These workers are banding together and using consensus to make sure nobody accepts jobs with poor conditions, or for less than is the industry-standard rate set by the workers.

And during the COVID-19 pandemic, it was clear where the relationship between the union and workers helped when it was desperately needed.

UNITED TECH AND ALLIED WORKERS

HOW TECH WORKERS ARE BUILDING TOOLS TO REBEL AGAINST SURVEILLANCE

> **MARCUS STORM, UTAW ORGANISER AND SPOKESPERSON**
>
> *"On union training courses, the undertone is very manager-worker divide. And as you know, in software, it's not like that anymore. If you work at a startup you might be a worker one day, you might be a manager the next day."*

United Tech and Allied Workers (UTAW) is a new union with a simple mission – to help build solidarity and networks among employees in tech workspaces.

It is a rather unique force for good in an industry where bosses have been allowed to go unchecked for many years – when you're in the machine, it can be hard to rage against it. Despite this, UTAW has attracted workers from industry giants such as Amazon, including its warehouses, Facebook, Twitter and Google, as well as those working in startups.

UTAW was founded in 2020, in association UK's Communication Workers Union (CWU) as a way to fill a gap in organising power that more traditional unions had not, so far, acknowledged. The idea was to help protect and advocate for a new wave of workers at historically inscrutable companies.

A key campaign for UTAW so far has been its 2021 effort to educate workers on employee surveillance – which came from demand from the network – but has a far wider reach than the tech industry.

According to a poll published by Prospect, in November 2021, one in three (32%) people were being monitored at work – up from a quarter (24%) just six months before. Younger workers (18 to 34) were found to be particularly at risk – 48% of younger workers said they were being monitored – including 20% being watched using cameras.[32] In one case the UTAW was involved in, employees were asked to switch their webcams on when working from home and if they were turned off, their management would ask why.

"We've got the Information Commissioner's Office (ICO) where hardly anybody knows about it," Marcus Storm, UTAW organiser and spokesperson, says. "They've got some vague guidance, which is not really actionable. And then you've got very, very, very little enforcement." The ICO is currently reviewing guidance to employers on the use of new technologies such as monitoring, but as with many things in tech, regulation is lagging behind the pace of change.

Through understanding the techniques CWU uses and linking up their own expertise, UTAW has bridged a crucial generational and skills-based gap. The campaign looks at what surveillance is, why and how it is used, how to combat it and what to do next if you feel your rights have been breached.

UTAW's website explains the first step to combating surveillance should come by enlisting the backing of a union:

> "Being part of a union means you will not face consequences alone: unions will provide you expertise and support you need, and may take your case all the way to court if necessary (without you having to hire expensive solicitors!). Your employer has money and a whole company on their side, so don't face them on your own: join a union!"

In the media, insurance firms, professional services and big banks, employees have all reported being monitored to see if they are at their desk, how much time they spend on messaging platforms, and through able hours.

Surveillance has also taken the shape of companies analysing employees' web activity, the movement of their cursor on the screen and even attention-tracking webcams, which monitor eye movement.

STARTING FROM SCRATCH

The union's creators designed and launched the project online during the COVID-19 pandemic, having first asked core questions: how do you organise in this space? How do you make sure that information gets to workers? How do you make sure workers understand their rights?

"In terms of unions, we didn't really see anything in the landscape, which was catering to tech workers, who are an example of a new kind of worker," says Storm. He cites union membership reaching an all-time low in the UK as evidence of a need for new organising spaces. The answer here lay in education campaigns and decentralised servers, among other things.

UTAW has found that many tech workplaces, particularly startups, simply aren't aware of some standard employment practices in the UK. Much of Storm's work as a rep has been about educating human-resources teams, and people who run companies, on the fairest ways to treat people, including consulting on issues related to working hours and holiday pay.

Storm believes the need for a union such as UTAW speaks to the new, sometimes ambiguous, structures we are seeing as the labour market evolves. He said there is scant information out there for people looking for answers independently.

"On union training courses, the undertone is very manager-worker divide. And as you know, in software, it's not like that anymore. If you work at a startup you might be a worker one day, you might be a manager the next day."

Using the expertise of its members, UTAW has also built its own state-of-the-art infrastructure in 'the cloud'. These new systems, Storm says, had to be safe and secure, and, crucially, not tied to big tech companies, such as Google.

Storm says the action the union has taken so far wouldn't have been possible without the technical expertise the organisation has within its membership. Many members have an in-depth understanding of coding and knowledge of what technology can do, as well as practical know-how on the different functionalities of systems and platforms.

Alongside the traditional functions of a union, part of its wider mission has also been to foster a sense of community – particularly as many of its members are remote workers – and partially to build support for its campaigns. UTAW has grown rapidly over the past 18 months and Storm says the majority of the membership is made up of young, white-collar software engineers – a significant portion of whom have never been in a union before.

It has a decentralised chat room online, where people talk about things like bikes and cooking, and the meetings are also less rigidly formal than some traditional unions. "We are very people-driven. If people want something, they ask, and we try to do our best to do it. We don't drive process," says Storm.

UTAW is now in the process of trying to build social, as well as professional networks, for organising across different companies.

A UNION OF THE OLD AND NEW

UTAW's setup shows how old and new unions can work together to support a changing workforce. It brings together organising and education power from the CWU, technical skills and flexibility of newer organisations.

Representing a highly-skilled workforce that can build the tools it needs puts this union in a rather privileged position – and the fact that this union didn't already exist – shows that technical skill is not the only thing that is needed to organise for change.

But the privilege that such engineers, and general white-collar tech workers, often hold within companies, as well as the financial compensation that goes alongside their jobs, makes them powerful. Now with greater collaboration and solidarity broader labour movement, can this power be used to help other sectors more widely?

Link: utaw.tech

THE FUNEMPLOYED

HOW A MINIMUM WAGE WAS SET BY A FACEBOOK GROUP

> BORIS FLETCHER, FUNEMPLOYED LONDON GROUP ADMIN
>
> *"It's an alternative to other middle men. You're in direct contact with employers, you're not going through an agency, you're not going through the job centre or anything like that."*

The events sector has perhaps always been a place where informal networks and connections are currency, with a proliferation of short-term 'gig' contracts and one-time arrangements.

FUNemployed is the name of a collection of Facebook groups that is premised on these conditions, for those working in the arts and events industries. The network has a cooperative ethos at its heart and its mantra is something of a modern labour exchange, which were, traditionally, government-funded places to help people find work.

Social networks, places where people gather, are natural places for organising around this kind of work, and these groups have been doing so now for a decade. Membership of the London group now stands at more than 18,000, as of the beginning of December 2021. Anywhere between 3 to 8 short term jobs or paid requests for gigs can be posted each day.

A minimum wage of £11 per hour is a minimum standard set by the administrators of the London group for all jobs posted. In one post, principal admin Boris Fletcher writes.

> "Well it seems the message is still not getting through, so from now on any post for work paid less than [the] group minimum of £11 per hour will see the member posting be removed from the group. There are simply no excuses for posting jobs which pay £9/hour."

> "Admin work hard to keep this group free of scammers and bots, there are over 5,000 dodgy profiles blocked on here so having to deal with unscrupulous employers is an added headache. We do this for free and ask for nothing except a little respect to all in the group."

> "Now bugger off and have a fantastic weekend funsters"

FUNemployed - London

Rules

1. **all membership questions must be answered**
   as above if you don't answer you won't be added i to the group

2. **Be kind and courteous**
   We're all in this together to create a welcoming environment. Let's treat everyone with respect. Healthy debates are natural, but kindness is required.

3. **Respect everyone's privacy**
   Being part of this group requires mutual trust. Authentic, expressive discussions make groups great, but may also be sensitive and private. What's shared in the group should stay in the group.

4. **no offensive language to other member**
   this includes swearing name calling and other types of abuse and or bullying it.WILL NOT BE TOLERATED OFFENDERS WILL BE BLOCKED

5. **Job and work posts**
   All jobs and work offered must include a description of work and rates of pay which must be a minimum of £11 per hour. Posts asking members to dm for job details will be removed,

6. **Only UK based members.**

7. **self promotion is allowed, but no spam.**

Screenshot, accessed 18/07/2022, FunEmployed

Other rules, such as being respectful of each other, working together and banning abuse, have followed on from that. Fletcher says the group generally runs itself. He rarely has to intervene, as the rules of the group are laid out and repeated regularly. If someone posts something that doesn't comply, they're asked to change it – if they don't change it – it doesn't get posted.

"I'll get maybe one or two posts a week where people advertise less than £11. Most people have got the message because I've repeated it and repeated it and repeated it," says Fletcher.

The minimum wage is going up to £12 in 2022, reflecting things like an exodus of people from the UK due to COVID-19 lockdowns and Brexit. As such, admins say they will be trailing this new message for two months ahead of the official change happening.

In this way, the network drives to help those working in unstable gig jobs get a better deal, as well as cutting out potentially unscrupulous intermediaries. "I think part of it is that it's an alternative to other middle men. You're in direct contact with employers, you're not going through an agency, you're not going through the job centre or anything like that," says Fletcher.

In this sense the group acts as a backstop for things like informal working arrangements that traditional unions might not be able to cover. Fletcher says that he believes many working in the gig economy do not see the benefit of joining a union when their work spans multiple agencies, companies or even industries.

"I think sometimes people don't realise what unions can and can't do as well, particularly what a union can do for you. Because people don't realise that unions give you full legal backup and things like that," says Fletcher.

AVOIDING THE CULT OF PERSONALITY

Fletcher says FUNemployed London was set up to emulate another Facebook group with similar aims. A rift had grown between the original founder and the other admins, says Fletcher, some people wanted change, and so spin-off groups of arts workers were formed in reaction.

"It was only 4,500 members when we took control four years ago," says Fletcher, who is a roadie for bands. "Since we started running it, it's been very, very different. I mean, some of the older members remembered the dirty old days."

Traditionally in unions there are democratic structures in place to ensure a cult of personality or factional rifts don't take hold – something that is difficult to replicate in Facebook groups. In a way, the group voted with their feet when they were dissatisfied with how previous groups had been run. With the new iterations of FUNemployed, a more collaborative and equal ethos took hold.

"One of our principal aims is that we don't accept any form of discrimination on the group. And anybody who does anything like that in the group generally gets removed. We re-built it partially because people know that they're not going to get abuse, and that they're not going to be told what and when they can do things.

"Because I came from the cooperative movement many years ago as part of a workers co-op back in the 80s, that's how I run it...everybody's equal."

The purpose of the group has evolved along membership, too, from exclusively events-based posts around music festivals, to things like people offering van transportation, as well as restaurant and bar work.

Despite a critical mass of people potentially being a target for the recruitment industry, Fletcher says there is no chance of the group being bought out by companies while he is running it, because of his cooperative principles.

The FUNemployed network shows how workers gaining control of the stream of work available and owning the way the work is distributed can help push up wages and improve conditions.

It also demonstrates how a cooperative approach can foster a community and network where people know they are getting a fair deal in a world where the traditionally unstable world of 'gig work' is the name of the game.

Link: www.facebook.com/groups/187489944721012 (the London group)

EVERYDOCTOR

14

HOW YOUNG MEDICS BUILT A NEW INSTITUTION AFTER THE JUNIOR DOCTORS' STRIKE

> DR EMILY GARDNER-BOUGAARD, EVERYDOCTOR MEMBER AND NHS WORKER
>
> *"Not everybody can do a trauma call. And not everybody can intubate someone. These are extreme examples, but a lot of people don't feel like saying, 'well, actually, yes, I think I should be paid more. And I should get my leave on time. And I should get maternity leave and not have to struggle and cry over it in order to get what is actually contractually obligated to me'."*

EveryDoctor is a campaigning organisation founded joint aims of fighting for a better NHS and improving working lives for its doctors.

Its action ranges from petitioning parliament and getting whistleblowers' stories safely into the press, to spearheading high-profile legal cases. Members join by committing to monthly payments and you can sign up to support whether you're a doctor or not.

The number of people paying to help the cause rose dramatically over the course of 2020 and 2021, as medics were put on the front lines of fighting the pandemic. But the seeds of EveryDoctor were sown in 2015 – as the UK's junior doctors were preparing to strike, in direct dispute with former health secretary Jeremy Hunt – all while the country was in the midst of Brexit fever.

The first four months of that year saw doctors from all specialties in England protesting contractual changes brought in by the government. Before this, there had only been one other strike carried out by NHS workers in the last 40 years – in 2012. To use a now-overused word, it was 'unprecedented'.

Doctors felt the new contracts being imposed on 'juniors' – those below the level of consultant – were unfair. A compromise deal, which at the time was said to be the government's final offer, was backed by the chair of the junior doctors' committee at the time, Dr Johann Malawana, in May 2016.

But Malawana resigned in July after British Medical Association (BMA) members voted against the agreement by 58% to 42%. His replacement, Dr Ellen McCourt, then said junior doctors would have no choice but to strike. Yet Hunt refused to engage in further meaningful negotiation.

In this moment, away from traditional union organising, a movement of doctors was galvanised – a Facebook group was set up, for doctors of all grades and specialities, which quickly gathered tens of thousands of members.

What has tended to be a rather conservative profession found a platform to air grievances, connect with others having similar issues, run polls to understand sentiment and campaign to make changes. EveryDoctor co-founder Dr Julia Patterson sees this as a turning point in how the profession viewed collective organising.

DOCTORS ORGANISING DOCTORS

"It's sort of frowned upon often in the senior echelons of the NHS to speak up about things like that and can be difficult for people," says Patterson. "But this moment showed very quickly how doctors could link up with one another and share news, share articles about what's going on," she adds. "And various projects were spearheaded off the back of that Facebook group, including one that myself and another doctor started."

EveryDoctor launched officially in 2019 and Patterson now works for the organisation full time, having taken a break from her speciality training to set it up. "Doctors find it quite difficult to mobilise in their places of work, because they work really extended hours and people move around quite a lot," says Patterson.

In particular, some junior doctors struggle to put down roots because they work in lots of different places for short periods of time. Alongside this, senior doctors often carry quite a weight of responsibility within their workplaces, meaning it can be difficult to build networks or speak up about problems."

Patterson sees EveryDoctor as an alternative space to the BMA, allowing medics to put a different kind of pressure on the government regarding crucial issues facing the profession. "I think the reason the community is so strong, and what we're doing resonates with doctors because they trust us stories they bring us. Because we really pay attention to their wellbeing, in ways doctors don't have in other places."

Aside from being a place for doctors to bring up issues they are facing, EveryDoctor is also seen as a complement to what Patterson calls the "medical establishment". Patterson says EveryDoctor tries to work with this powerful force, supporting unions in acting fast where injustices are felt.

"What we've actually been finding over COVID, certainly, is that organisations such as ours are small, very responsive and able to mobilise people very quickly, are able to feed into the broader ecosystem of activism, and the BMA certainly is responding to that," says Patterson.

The group has found a kind of symbiosis BMA. As EveryDoctor reacts quickly, getting voices into the media and creating campaigns, the BMA backs this up with surveys and public statements.

RETURNING THE LOVE FOR THE JOB

On an individual level, it has helped people find their voice within the profession too. Dr Emily Gardner-Bougaard says she joined the cause because she and her colleagues were having issues, such as being denied booked leave or sympathy leave, and not being paid properly. When she had taken grievances to the BMA in the past, they had told her these decisions are made on a trust-by-trust basis.

"It wasn't so much the job – I love being a doctor – but it's the work environment that goes with it," says Gardner-Bougaard. "And you really felt that you weren't being represented, or people weren't really listening and trying to do something about your problems. People just felt like they weren't heard and they weren't empowered."

Particularly during the pandemic, across the country, emergency staff rotas were put into effect without much discussion with or pushback from the BMA.

"Not everybody can do a trauma call. And not everybody can intubate someone. These are extreme examples, but a lot of people don't feel like saying, 'well, actually, yes, I think I should be paid more. And I should get my leave on time. And I should get maternity leave and not have to struggle and cry over it in order to get what is actually contractually obligated to me'."

Taking on this kind of organising hasn't come without scrutiny – some doctors believe the name 'EveryDoctor' presents the organisation as more representative of the profession than it actually is. Its leaders aren't elected, as they might be in a traditional union, and there's something of a reliance on social-media presence and retweets, meaning its messages have to resonate among the noise in people's feeds.

Nevertheless, EveryDoctor has shown how grassroots campaigning, and doing things a bit differently, can make important changes that might not be otherwise possible. It has brought the profession together in ways they would never have been able to previously.

It is a rare example of something that started out as a Facebook group and has morphed into a membership organisation with considerable success. Paid membership hit around 1,700 by mid-2021, from around 500 members at the start of 2020. But the network is much larger when taking into account vast social-media followings on Twitter and Facebook.

This effort also shows the power that can be created when old unions and digitally savvy new organisations work together.

The organisation is currently having to think about where it can go next – as younger people migrate from Facebook onto different platforms such as Instagram or TikTok – and it looks to expand its audience. "You don't want to become an organisation that represents one type of doctor of a certain age," says Patterson.

While it thinks about its future, it could be a good blueprint for other campaigning groups looking to make the leap from online campaigning to a more formal structure.

Link: www.everydoctor.org.uk

#FREELANCERPAYGAP AND JOURNO RESOURCES

EPILOGUE: HOW WRITERS ARE BUILDING POWER BY POOLING DATA

LUCY HARLEY-MCKEOWN

"Contributing my own rates made me feel like I was part of a movement helping future freelance writers navigate the industry. I felt networked and part of the workforce, rather than just a solo agent with no backup."

It's considered bad practice for journalists to make themselves the story, so forgive me for writing about my own experience of navigating the labour market for a moment.

My career has been coloured by ubiquitous short-term contracts in both publishing and journalism, confusion about my rights and, initially, a lack of good information about what it means to be self-employed. For the final part of this book, I wanted to break down something that has affected nearly every kind of workplace and workforce – something that millions of people are vulnerable to.

When I first went freelance back in March 2020, I'd had my contract with my previous employer terminated with two weeks' notice, as was their right to do. I was thrust into freelancing during one of the deepest recessions of my working lifetime, alongside many others. It was pandemic pandemonium, and I was without any right to redundancy pay or furlough. Freelance support from the government was only extended to a subset of those that had been self-employed for more than two years.

Previously, when working in publishing, I had been on semi-precarious 'rolling' contracts. These are often used by employers in the UK to protect budgets and because, after two years of constant employment from one company, workers are entitled to certain rights.

It's in the interest of employers, therefore, not to keep contractors on for more than two years, lest they have to consider things such as redundancy pay. Any employee on a fixed-term contract for four or more years will automatically become a permanent employee, unless the employer can show there is a good business reason that they can't do this.

Despite being in the National Union of Journalists (NUJ), as a freelancer, I spent a lot of time wondering about the correct amount to charge, whether I had undervalued myself and if negotiating would ever get easier. No editor ever tells you the correct price range straight up. In an industry that, in some ways, is strapped for cash, everyone is looking to get a good deal.

There is also the hazard of potentially undercutting the market if you undercharge, which can bring down future rates for everyone else. The depressing fact is that in journalism, people routinely work for free or for low pay, churning out potentially regrettable opinion pieces for a pittance and often falling back on family wealth.

Meanwhile, despite being useful for helping navigate legal rights and terms in contracts, the NUJ's advice on fees, and the freelance section of its website, seemingly hadn't been updated for decades. Although the essence of the advice offered is correct, it feels like shaky ground to start from.

Luckily for me, over the last few years, there has been growing attention paid to the employment rights of journalists, as well as historic wins in terms of union representation. In July 2019, Vice workers unionised, with bosses at the youth-focused website choosing to voluntarily recognise their staff's right to form a negotiating unit. This decision followed four months of discussions involving employees and the NUJ in the UK.

15 - #FREELANCERPAYGAP AND JOURNO RESOURCES

Other news workers have also started to organise, including staff at The New Yorker, and separately Buzzfeed News in the US coming together to demand better rights.

BUILDING UP SHARED WORKER RESOURCES

Alongside such change inside publications, many independent resources for freelance journalists and people in the creative industries have materialised. One is a crowdsourced freelance writing rate spreadsheet, which the creators suggest amounts to a database representing the 'freelance pay gap'.

Masterminded by Anna Codrea-Rado, Alex Holder and Vikki Ross, the spreadsheet aims to capture data on wage disparities in journalism, public speaking and the advertising industry. It was shared on Twitter and gained visibility hashtag #FreelancePayGap. When the project launched, Codrea-Rado tweeted:

> *"We all know the* #FreelancerPayGap *exists but no one tracks it. Share your rates & change that."*

Information collected includes age, years spent in the industry, gender identity, ethnicity, how much you were paid for a particular project and whether the work was secured through a pre-existing relationship. As of the end of 2021, it had more than 850 entries.

It offered a lifeline for those trying to negotiate work during the pandemic and acts as a 'living resource', more dynamic than much of the work the NUJ has done since I have been a member. Contributing my own rates to it made me feel like I was part of a movement helping future freelance writers navigate the industry. I felt networked and part of the workforce, rather than just a solo agent with no backup.

Alongside this, there are now multitudes of Facebook groups and websites dedicated to calling out bad employers, giving tips on negotiation and sharing resources, as well as newsletters advertising paid opportunities.

One such space is Journo Resources. This is a website started by Jem Collins out of frustration that she couldn't find anywhere collating job opportunities, pay information and advice in an accessible format for modern journalists. Part of the website is dedicated to sharing up-to-date day rates for work, such as news reporting and sub-editing.

15 - #FREELANCERPAYGAP AND JOURNO RESOURCES

"For me it felt like the simplest thing to do was create resources, rather than try to restructure a whole organisation such as the NUJ, which sort of felt like it catered to an older demographic," says Collins.

Journo Resources had its fifth birthday in 2021, around the same time as Collins' full-time job became managing the website. Funded through donations and a paid-for jobs board, the site also runs a well-regarded jobs newsletter. It has amassed nearly 20,000 followers on Twitter.

Facebook groups have also sprung up in support of journalists around the world. One such group is a women-only Facebook group where PRs and journalists can ask questions about rates, pitch stories and build their networks. Another is geared towards students and those with less experience. There's also one that connects international journalists with editors who need stories and services from specific locations.

Despite its reputation for union busting, Slack was also a key tool connecting people when much of the world shut down in March 2020. The Society of Freelance Journalists (SFJ) was founded in response to the pandemic and it quickly amassed more than 1,000 members around the world. That has since doubled.

The SFJ directors and founding members – Laura Oliver, Abigail Edge, Caroline Harrap and John Crowley – volunteer their time to maintain and develop the group, driven by their collective goal to support and lend a voice to this fast-growing part of the media industry.

A CATALYST FOR CHANGE?

Many of the structures created and maintained by freelance journalists over the course of the pandemic were built with accountability in mind. Working alone can be an isolating experience. Different initiatives have shown how building networks among workers, who may feel naturally in competition with each other, can help them drive out bad actors and drive up conditions for everyone.

Many tools and resources that now exist demonstrate how a union such as the NUJ could try to harness the power of the crowd and this collective energy. For many, entering their wages in a group spreadsheet can be the first step towards more formal union membership.

My experience aside, the precariousness that comes with being a freelance journalist has bigger consequences. According to the Pew Research Center,[33] in the US, newspaper newsroom employment fell by more than half between 2008 and 2020, from roughly 71,000 roles to about 31,000. That's a big decrease in

15 - #FREELANCERPAYGAP AND JOURNO RESOURCES

stable jobs within a workforce seen by some as critical for holding power to account.

In a world of misinformation, disinformation, lobbying, unregulated tech platforms, questionable government spending, wars, health emergencies, rising seas and temperatures, and more – structures that support the people that attempt to get us accurate and reliable information, and uncover the most uncomfortable truths – could make all the difference.

Links: docs.google.com/spreadsheets/d/1GajDnwJHg-WDzNnaZRmi8eoZtaV5A8NZqLV8l_aKJf08
www.journoresources.org.uk

GLOSSARY

Algorithm: *A process or set of rules to be followed in calculations or other problem-solving operations, especially by a computer.*

Artificial Intelligence (AI): *The theory and development of computer systems able to perform tasks normally requiring human intelligence, such as visual perception, speech recognition, decision-making, and translation between languages.*

Application Programming Interface (API): *A software intermediary that allows two applications to talk to each other.*

Bootstrapping: *To get (oneself or something) into or out of a situation using existing resources.*

Clickworker: *Someone who gains their income by clicking on software to test it for bugs or problems.*

The Cloud: *Servers that are accessed over the Internet, and the software and databases that run on those servers.*

Crowdsource: *Obtain (information or input into a particular task or project) by enlisting the services of a large number of people, either paid or unpaid, typically via the internet.*

Crowdwork: *The execution of work by a large number of people who each contribute a small amount of labour.*

C-suite: *A term used to describe high-ranking executive titles in an organisation.*

Decentralised: The delegation of power from a central authority to multiple smaller stakeholders.

Gig economy: *A free market system in which temporary positions are common and organizations hire independent workers for short-term commitments. Often used to describe new forms of work that can be mediated by platforms such as driving for Uber.*

Google Docs: *An online free word processor created by Google which allows many different users to edit or write in the document at the same time from different places.*

GDPR: *The General Data Protection Regulation (GDPR) is a legal framework that sets guidelines for the collection and processing of personal information from individuals who live in the European Union (EU).*

Influencer: *A person who has the power to affect the purchasing decisions of others because of his or her authority, knowledge, position, or relationship with his or her audience. Influencers often enter paid marketing partnerships with brands to sell products to their followers.*

Inflation: *A general increase in prices and fall in the purchasing value of money.*

Plug-in: *A software component that adds a specific feature to an existing programme or service.*

Reddit: An American social news aggregation,content rating, and discussion website. Registered users submit content to the site's forums such as links, text posts, images, and videos, which are then voted up or down by other members.

Self-employed: *Working for oneself as a freelance or the owner of a business rather than for an employer.*

Subject Access Request: *A legal request from an individual to access and receive a copy of their personal data, and other supplementary information held by a body, company or organisation.*

Subreddit: *A particular forum on Reddit is known as a subreddit. You can have subreddits for news, hobbies and many other things.*

Viral hashtag: *Hashtags are words or multi-word phrases that categorize content and track topics on Twitter, Facebook, Instagram and other networks. If you look up a hashtag you will see all the content that has been produced in relation to that topic. A viral hashtag is a hashtag that is circulating rapidly and widely on the internet.*

Zero-hours contract: *Zero-hour contract is a term used to describe a type of employment contract between an employer and an employee whereby the employer is not obliged to provide any minimum number of working hours to the employee.*

ACKNOWLEDGEMENTS

This project wouldn't have seen the light of day without my friends and family. They witnessed many crises of confidence, brought support when I had run out of steam, and told me to take a break when things weren't working, and sometimes confiscated my digital devices.

In no order, thanks to: Mum, Dad, Sophie, Tom, Elsie, Mark, Katy, Polly, Berengere, Mischa, Charlie, Elliot, Ed, Robyn, Will, Elyse, Lola, Tom.

Sometimes, when writing, time is a flat circle, but Hannah and Ed kept the wheels on the track. They also provided many of the case studies, context and gave a rudder to the narrative as a whole. Thanks also to John Wood from the TUC for his advice and suggestions.

Thanks to Labour Together and Compass for funding this project, as well as for commissioning the original

New Power newsletter this book was borne out of. Thanks also to Jon Cruddas MP for writing a generous and thoughtful foreword.

The people I interviewed will always have my solidarity for being defiant, ingenious and indefatigable.

NOTES

[1] Taylor, Matthew, Good work: the Taylor review of modern working practices   *https://www.gov.uk/government/publications/good-work-the-taylor-review-of-modern-working-practices,* accessed 4 June 2022.

[2] Bradley, Chris & Stumpner, Peter, The impact of Covid-19 on capital markets, McKinsey https://www.mckinsey.com/business-functions/strategy-and-corporate-finance/our-insights/the-impact-of-covid-19-on-capital-markets-one-year-in, accessed 4 June 2022.

[3] "Terrifying prospect" of over a quarter of a ion more people crashing intreme levels of poverty and suffering this year, Oxfam https://www.oxfam.org/en/press-releases/terrifying-prospect-over-quarter-ion-more-people-crashing-extreme-levels-poverty, accessed 4 June 2022.

[4] New Economics Foundation Spring Statement analysis, https://neweconomics.org/2022/03/spring-statement-leaves-48-of-all-children-living-in-families-that-have-to-make-sacrifices-on-essentials-this-spring-like-putting-food-on-the-table-or-replacing-clothes-and-shoes, accessed 4 June 2022.

[5] Retail sales, Great Britain: November 2021, Office for National Statistics, https://www.ons.gov.uk/businessindustryandtrade/retailindustry/bulletins/retailsales/november 2021, accessed 4 June 2022.

[6] Gig economy 'on course to surge 300% in three years', AppJobs, https://businesscloud.co.uk/news/gig-economy-on-course-to-surge-300-

in-three-years/, accessed 4 June 2022.

[7] What does the rise of self-employment tell us about the UK labour market?, Institute for Fiscal Studies, https://ifs.org.uk/publications/15182, accessed June 2022.

[8] Osborne, Hilary, The Guardian, Home workers putting in more hours since Covid, research shows https://www.theguardian.com/business/2021/feb/04/home-workers-putting-in-more-hours-since-covid-research, accessed 4 June 2022.

[9] Novitz, Tonia (September 2002). "A Revised Role for Trade Unions as Designed by New Labour: The Representation Pyramid and 'Partnership'". Journal of Law and Society. 29 (3): 487–509. doi:10.1111/1467-6478.00229. Retrieved 21 July 2021.

[10] UK Department for Business, Energy & Industrial Strategy, Trade Union Membership, UK 1995-2020: Statistical Bulletin https://assets.publishing.service.gov.uk/government/uploads/system/uploads/attachment_data/file/989116/Trade-union-membership-2020-statistical-bulletin.pdf, accessed 5 June 2022.

[11] Weil, David, The Fissured Workplace, Harvard University Press, 2017.

[12] Livingstone, Eve, Make Bosses Pay: Why we need unions, Pluto Books, 2021.

[13] Reddit https://www.reddit.com/r/mturk/comments/91ky29/i_love_you_guys_and_turkopticon_so_much/, accessed 4 June 2022.

[14] Irani, Lilly C and Silberman, M. Six, Turkopticon: Interrupting Worker Invisibility in Amazon Mechanical Turk http://crowdsourcing-class.org/readings/downloads/ethics/turkopticon.pdf, accessed 4 June 2022.

[15] Reddit https://www.reddit.com/r/mturk/comments/ecq8bp/its_insulting_as_fuck_when_requesters_want_you_to/, accessed 4 June 2022.

[16] Turkopticon, Guidelines for Academic Requesters, PDF version https://cpb-us-e1.wpmucdn.com/sites.northwestern.edu/dist/2/2819/files/2020/01/guidelinesforacademicrequesters-1.pdf, accessed 5 June 2022.

[17] Turkopticon, Guidelines for Academic Requesters https://blog.

NOTES

turkopticon.net/?page_id=121, accessed 5 June 2022.

[18] MIT Culture Index https://sloanreview.mit.edu/culture500, accessed 4 June 2022.

[19] National Gallery: N27 group win workers' rights, BBC News, https://www.bbc.co.uk/news/uk-england-london-47409755, accessed 4 June 2022.

[20] Tan, Gillian, Bloomberg https://www.bloomberg.com/news/articles/2021-07-30/robo-lawyer-valued-at-210-million-with-backing-from-andreessen, accessed 4 June 2022.

[21] Uber BV and others (Appellants) V Aslam and others (Respondents), Supreme Court judgment https://www.supremecourt.uk/cases/uksc-2019-0029.html, accessed 5 June 2022.

[22] Grady, Constance, Black Authors are on Bestseller Lists Right Now. But Publishing Doesn't Pay them Enough, Vox, https://www.vox.com/culture/2020/6/17/21285316/publishing-paid-me-diversity-black-authors-systemic-bias, accessed 4 June 2022.

[23] #PublishingPaidMe Google spreadsheet https://docs.google.com/spreadsheets/d/1Xsx6rKJtafa8f_prlYYD3zRxaXYVDaPXbasvt_iA2vA/edit#gid=1798364047, accessed 4 June 2022.

[24] An update on HBG's diversity and inclusion efforts, Hachette Book Group https://www.hachettebookgroup.com/corporate-social-responsibility/an-update-on-diversity-may-2021/, accessed 4 June 2022.

[25] Penguin Random House U.S. Publishing Programs Audit Findings, Penguin Random House https://authornews.penguinrandomhouse.com/penguin-random-house-u-s-publishing-programs-audit-findings/, accessed 4 June 2022.

[26] 20 Surprising Influencer Marketing Statistics, Digital Marketing institute https://digitalmarketinginstitute.com/blog/20-influencer-marketing-statistics-that-will-surprise-you, accessed 4 June 2022.

[27] 2020 Influencer Pricing Report, Klear https://klear.com/Influencer-Rates2020.pdf, accessed 4 June 2022.

[28] Lorenz, Taylor, The App Unprintable Name That Wants to Give Power to Creators, The New York Times https://www.nytimes.com/2021/08/02/technology/fypm-creators-app-pay.html, accessed 4 June 2022.

[29] What are wages like in the legal sector?, Organise https://the.organise.network/surveys/legal-aid-wages, accessed 5 June

[30] Cooper, David & Kroeger, Teresa, Employers steal ions from workers' paychecks each year, Economic Policy Institute https://www.epi.org/publication/employers-steal-ions-from-workers-paychecks-each-year/, accessed 5 June 2022.

[31] Clark, Nick & Herman, Eva, Unpaid Britain: wage default in the British labour market, Trust for London https://www.trustforlondon.org.uk/publications/unpaid-britain-wage-default-british-labour-market/, accessed 5 June 2022.

[32] New protections needed to stop employer surveillance of remote workers, Prospect https://prospect.org.uk/news/new-protections-needed-to-stop-employer-surveillance-of-remote-workers/, accessed 5 June.

[33] Walker, Mason, U.S. newsroom employment has fallen 26% since 2008, Pew Research Center https://www.pewresearch.org/fact-tank/2021/07/13/u-s-newsroom-employment-has-fallen-26-since-2008/#:~:text=Newspaper%20newsroom%20employment%20fell%2057,to%20about%2018%2C000%20in%202020, accessed 4 June 2022.